Eastward Toward Eve

EASTWARD
TOWARD
EVE

A Geography of Soul

by
MADONNA KOLBENSCHLAG

A Crossroad Book
Crossroad Publishing Company
New York

1996
The Crossroad Publishing Company
370 Lexington Avenue, New York, NY 10017

Printed in the United States of America

Library of Congress Cataloging-in-Publication Data

Kolbenschlag, Madonna, 1935–
    Eastward toward Eve : a geography of soul / by Madonna
Kolbenschlag.
        p.   cm.
    Includes bibliographical references.
    ISBN 0-8245-1579-X (pbk.)
    1. Women and religion.   2. Woman (Theology)   3. East and West.
    4. Sex role – Religious aspects.   5. Man–woman relationships.   6. Man
(Theology)   7. Myth.   I. Title.
    BL458.K65   1996
    305.3–dc20   96-5365
                                                                  CIP

For Paul and Erika and Helen

Contents

Acknowledgments ix

Introduction 1

Chapter

1 Eclipse of the Feminine:
The Repressed Anima in Culture and Psyche 5

2 God and Self: The One and the Many 23

3 Gender Masks and the Third Sex 46

4 Encounters with the "Other":
The "Yang" of Teilhard de Chardin
and Thomas Merton 67

5 Journey into Difference:
The "Yin" of Mary Catherine Bateson,
Audre Lorde, and Joanna Macy 90

6 In Search of Eve and Our True Mother 110

Afterword 135

Notes 136

Acknowledgments

No one can write a book without incurring a huge debt to many others—some for their timely assistance, some for their listening ear, and some simply for their understanding patience.

I am grateful to my publisher, Mike Leach, for all of the above. Without Paul McGrath and Keiko Noguchi of Japan, this journey could not have been possible. I treasure their friendship, insight, and determination to introduce me to Japanese readers. The hospitality they and their colleagues of the Aichi Prefectural University of Nagoya and the Nagoya Gakuin University extended to me was extraordinary. I am also indebted to Takeko Minami and Akihide Mizutani for their generous help with translation of some of my correspondence and resources.

Finally, I express my profound gratitude for all those who have appreciated, supported, and nourished my gift as a writer over these many years. Without them, I would not have the voice or vision to create and continue this dialog with the world.

Introduction

This book began as a series of lectures that I gave in Japan in November of 1994. I had gone to Japan to speak and dialog about issues of common interest, in particular the interest generated by my books *Kiss Sleeping Beauty Good-Bye* and *Lost in the Land of Oz*. When I returned I realized that my first encounter with an Asian culture was only the beginning of a journey I had to continue, a journey into "difference."

In all the other cultures I had visited previously there was always something familiar—the language, the character of the people, the customs, sometimes the religious tradition. In Japan, in spite of the superficial veneer of modernization and Americanization, I discovered that the inner soul of Japan was very different from the soul of the West.

At times I was absolutely charmed by the differences, at times puzzled, and at other times made intensely aware of things in myself that could not assimilate the difference. My conversations and lectures focused on the relationship of myth to culture and gender, and the significance of the changes in the self-perception of women in our era. The myths of masculinity and femininity, and the gendered nature of consciousness, are pathways into the geography of the modern soul.

My first book, *Kiss Sleeping Beauty Good-Bye*, will soon be available to Japanese readers, in the fifth language since its publication in 1979. This continuing "reincarnation" is evidence that awareness of the changing feminine consciousness is a trans-cultural, global phenomenon. Something is happening that tran-scends our differences, that is struggling to provide us with a common language of understanding, a way of *seeing* that will guide us into the future.

On the long flight home I realized that the dialog begun in Japan would continue, not only because of the social and political changes and challenges of our time, but because it echoed a dialog going on in my own soul. Something deep inside me was in the process of recognizing and integrating parts of myself that had remained buried or muted by almost sixty years of enculturation and experience. The exploration of this inner geography of con-sciousness is a kind of bass accompaniment to the treble notes that are stirring the intercultural dialog today.

The starting point for me on this journey into difference has been my interest in and insight into the gendered nature of power and culture. For many years I have understood the categories and phenomena of "masculine" and "feminine" as metaphors for the way that power and values are constellated in the social order. From another perspective, the categories of "East" and "West" have provided a shorthand for the way in which psychological, spir-itual, and social qualities are differentiated in our civilization. Sometimes the double set of polarities overlaps. These polarities are *myths* that have shaped our world in ways that we are just begin-ning to comprehend, even as these myths undergo profound trans-formation.

Pursuing this inner and outer dialog made it necessary to find a language that could make sense of both. Realizing that our contem-porary way of life suppresses important parts of ourselves at the same time that it cordons off parts of our common human experi-ence, I searched for a language that could interpret these differ-ences. I discovered a useful hybrid in adapting both Jung's and the feminist views of "the unconscious."

Since I find it impossible to separate the personal and the cul-tural dimensions of consciousness, the reader will experience this bifocal perspective throughout this book. What I offer is a series of essays, each of which stands alone or with the rest. This is a book of reflections on the "masculine" and the "feminine" and on the "East" and the "West" as double threads that weave our human destiny, a kind of cultural DNA or double helix that winds through our individual and collective reality, creating consciousness and demanding our attention.

The experience recorded here raises important questions: Is there a point of convergence, a balance that we must approach? What is the wisdom that will finally free us from our self-destructive ways?

If we do not undertake the journey into *difference* we may never be able to answer these questions. We may never discover the geography of our own soul or recognize the contours of our world. The geography of soul is a vast territory; part of it is visible and conscious to us, and part is hidden, unconscious or unlived, perhaps rejected. The only way we can find our way into and through this territory is through some experience of what we are not, or of what we have chosen not to be. *Difference* is our compass.

I invite the reader to play with these ideas and embark on this journey into *seeing* and *reimagining* ourselves and our world.

December 10, 1995

∽

Chapter One

Eclipse of the Feminine: The Repressed Anima in Culture and Psyche

Each of us has a unique, personal story—the story of how we came to be who we are. And we also have a collective story, a larger story that encompasses the individual life and molds us into a people, a culture. These stories, personal as well as collective, are often referred to as *myths*.

Myths provide a framework for interpreting experience, for making sense of the world and choosing a response. Myths offer ways of ordering experience; they give us insight about ourselves and a defense against chaos. They describe a scenario for human action and give meaning to our common history. These narrative metaphors are imprinted on our consciousness like fingerprints: they are practically indelible, and, as evidence increasingly demonstrates, they may also be genetic.

Over the passage of time, experience is converted into myth: First, there is *experience,* "something happens"; then there is a *response* or *adaptation,* "something responds." This response or adaptation is successful, "it works," and therefore is remembered and becomes a *precedent.* Repetition of similar experiences and responses reinforce the precedent, and structures are invented to perpetuate it : thus follows *institutionalization.* Religion and other social imperatives such as law give the precedent a preferred status. This *legitimation* begins to model human expectations. Finally "it" becomes "me" through the process of *internalization.*[1]

This is the process by which, as individuals, we are "enculturated" into a "mythology" that has the power to legitimate and censor, to transform energy and consciousness. Culture has been defined as "a constellation of compelling metaphors," the "supernatural charter" on which a society is based. At the personal level, it becomes a kind of shorthand for the process by which culturally defined meaning and motivation are structured into our consciousness.[2]

Cultural myths develop in diverse ways. For example, the myth of America developed from a process of accretion of many New World myths which predated the "institutionalization" during the Colonial and Revolutionary periods. Some cultures are rooted in a foundational myth of a "curse," the result of a moral offense against a divinity. The Celtic myth of Macha, a goddess abused and outraged by her male competitors, is imprinted in many ways in the ethos of the Irish culture.[3] Some regard the Judaeo-Christian civilization also as the child of a "curse," namely, the Fall and the loss of Eden.

Creation stories are an extraordinary reservoir of myth. Such stories are a good starting point for understanding ourselves as well as those who are different from us. Two questions prick our curiosity: (1) What in these stories might explain *difference*? and (2) What do the stories have in common? These questions are particularly interesting in any attempt to explain culturally determined concepts such as "feminine" and "masculine," "East" and "West."

Quite possibly the oldest creation myth of Western civilization is first recorded in the Babylonian epic *Enuma Elish*. The version we have today dates to around 2000 B.C. but had its origin in a Sumerian oral tradition that was much earlier. Most of the Near Eastern (later, Western) myths that were recorded date from a time when the preeminence of the Great Mother was waning as the symbolic center of civilization and many of her functions were delegated to her male consort or son. The appearance of the usurping warrior heroes in most of these cultures corresponds with the establishment of a patriarchal order, the suppression of the religions of the Great Mother, and the devaluation of the feminine.

The story of Tiamat and Marduk in the *Enuma Elish* is a paradigm of the birth of Western civilization. Tiamat was the Mother of the Deep, who fashioned all things. She was before all. Tiamat mated with her spouse, Apsu (the waters), and gave birth to the junior gods. But her progeny fought among themselves. Apsu was displeased with the rebellious behavior of the gods and wanted to destroy them. But Tiamat counseled patience. The young males, out of fear, killed Apsu. Tiamat threatened vengeance. The wisest of the young warrior gods proposed to meet Tiamat and wage peace. But because of his fear he could not confront her, and the strategy was abandoned.

Marduk, the most aggressive upstart, boasted with defiant arrogance that he would destroy Tiamat. He mocked her femaleness as weakness. He plotted to assure his own ultimate supremacy by killing off his rivals, then entered into an epic battle with Tiamat, who had transformed herself into a raging sea monster. Marduk vanquished her by driving the violent winds through her body. Afterward, he pondered what to do with her carcass. In a stroke of patriarchal genius, he divided her in half, then fragmented the corpse. He used the pieces to construct the universe.

This primordial act of matricidal dismemberment is one myth that interprets the symbolic foundation and political ethos of the Western world. The Great Mother, the fountain of immanent life, is transformed into something dark, chaotic, and evil. The sun-god brings life to the world by killing the Mother serpent, the dragon of darkness. Out of the dismembered corpse of the Great Mother rises a new order.

The story of Tiamat's mutilation and displacement is repeated in other cultures, for example, in the myth of the goddess Tlalteuctli from the Nahuatl people of pre-Aztec Mexico. Tlalteuctli is assaulted by the male gods Quetzalcoatl and Tezcatlipoca while walking alone over the primordial deep. She is ripped apart, and her body parts are used to create the world.

Marduk, too, has many successors, including Yahweh in Genesis. The eradication of the goddess from Judaism and Christianity is very explicit. Tiamat, and all of the other names attributed to her, is the primordial name for the serpentine spirit of earth and its underground waters. The serpent is associated with the power of the Great Mother and with the sea, the source of life. In Genesis the serpent is banished from the garden as a source of moral evil. The final extinction of the dragon is promised in the book of Revelation (12:21) when a messiah-king kills the oceanic snake and assumes unchallenged power over the world. The serpent myth has many descendants: the sun-worshiping pharaohs of Egypt slay the dragon Apophys; Apollo slays the python of Gaia; Perseus slays the Medusa; St. George slays the dragon in Britain and in Russia; St. Patrick drives the snakes from Ireland.

The creation myth of Tiamat and Marduk illustrates the theological psychology of our civilization: competition, combat, victory, individuality, creation from the spoils, and power over. The scenario repeats over and over in our history. A generation of cowards refuses to honor and negotiate with the primordial Mother; a warrior hero represses and oppresses female-identified energies in himself, in others, in nature. The suppressed energies turn into cultural pathogens. The hero makes the feminine inert and literally creates the world out of its fragmented energy.

When we turn to the creation myths of the Far East, there is considerable evidence that the stories are less monolithic in their meaning and significance. In Chinese and Japanese mythology, the creation stories are less personal, more ambiguous, and certainly not monotheistic. The cosmogonies of the *I Ching*, of Lao Tzu, and of Confucius were impersonal. One senses the interplay of fundamental forces, *Yin* and *Yang*, but no hegemony of huge personae or egos. Much later than in the Indo-European myths, divine personae emerge, but they are more benign, and no force is completely obliterated, no persona is violently eliminated.

One late Chinese creation story shows the contrast. Nu Kua (also called Nu Wa or Nu Hsi). She (or he, for the sex is indeterminate in some versions) is said to have had the body of a serpent and a human head, to have molded the earth and created man, but was not the sole creator. Later a rebel arose, and in the ensuing struggle the "pillars" of heaven and the "corners" of the earth were destroyed. Nu Kua repaired the heavens and rebuilt the foundations of the earth.

In the Honan province today there is a month-long Renzu Festival in honor of Nu Wa and her male brother-consort Fuxi. Before the Han period, the two deities had independent myths. Nu Wa formed the earth, created humans, patched the heavens together. She presided over marriages and fertility. Over time, the patriarchal development of Chinese culture seems to have submerged Nu Wa into Fuxi, so that many temples once dedicated to her were destroyed and not rebuilt after the Cultural Revolution. At the Renzu Festival in Huaiyang it is quite clear that although Fuxi is the dominant deity, the chief customs and ceremonies are directed to Nu Wa.[4]

The most traditional and popular Japanese creation story shows a conspicuous absence of a supreme divine persona. Out of the primal sea a divine substance emerges that sprouts many "reed shoots" and is regarded as a pluriform deity. Two other divine creatures participate in the trio, which gives birth to generations of deities known as "kami." Shinto, the indigenous Japanese mythology, regards every natural thing—human or animal, plant or tree, volcano or waterfall—as possessing, in varying degrees, a "kami" or divine spirit. The primal male (Izanagi) and the primal female (Izanami), "brother" and "sister" deities, eventually create much of the natural landscape of Japan as well as the rest of the Shinto pantheon. After Izanami dies giving birth, she goes to the underworld, and mortal life and death are forever divided. Their progeny, another brother and sister, Amaterasu, the Sun Goddess, and Susano, the Storm God, are a pale reflection of Tiamat and Marduk. When Susano humiliates Amaterasu, she hides in a cave and the sun is darkened. She emerges only when the goddess of mirth makes a festivity and Amaterasu sees her reflection in a mirror outside the cave. Light is restored. Neither is destroyed.

As in many of the Far Eastern legends and stories, in the creation stories of the Native American nations the patriarchal displacement of the feminine is not so violent or complete. Many of the Native American stories of creation actually recognize a supreme female creator, such as Thought Woman, or Spider Woman, or Changing Woman. The story of White Buffalo Calf Woman picks up a familiar thread—the disappearance and promised reappearance of the feminine.

In almost every mythological system of our global civilization one can find some evidence of this common thread: themes that suggest an eclipse of the feminine. The creative female principle of energy is displaced, oppressed or offended, violated or fragmented, driven into hiding, forced underground.

The Judaeo-Christian creation story in Genesis provides an interesting variation in the scenario. Yahweh, of course, is the archetypal supreme god—judgmental, punitive, wrathful, all-powerful in the hierarchy of being, one who will have "no other gods" before him. Indeed, Yahweh seems to have displaced Sophia, the creatrix deity, who preceded him. Another disappearing feminine presence is Adam's female companion Lilith, who preceded Eve. Lilith was banished into the wilderness because she would not be submissive to Adam, would not line up in the pecking order established by Yahweh. Eve appears as a kind of "scab" and subsequently is blamed for the entrance of evil into the world and is made subservient to Adam.

Depending on whether your interpretation of myth is more anthropological or psychological, this common thread of the eclipse of the feminine can be seen as fossil evidence of the rise of patriarchy at a particular time in history and the consequent displacement of a symbolic as well as real order of power associated with the feminine principle of life. A more psychological view, which does not necessarily exclude the anthropological view, might interpret it as an artifact of the complementary nature of the sexes or as evidence of a primordial awe and fear of the power of the feminine.

Jung's concepts of *archetype* and the *collective unconscious* provide an interesting psychological framework for understanding the eclipse of the feminine. By examining his patients' dreams, Jung discovered that the spontaneous imagery of the mind fell into patterns that resembled myth, legend, and fairytale, and that this material did not originate in personal perceptions, memory, or conscious experience. Eventually, because of the ubiquity of these images (at least among Europeans), he concluded that there is a part of the psyche that is held in common, and he named it the *collective unconscious*.

This collective unconscious is made up of a constellation of *archetypes*, which he described as norms, instincts, or patterns of psychological activity. His theory of the process by which they are formed is analogous to the theory of how myths develop sociologically, as described previously. Jung claimed that certain fundamental experiences occur and are repeated over millions of years. Such experiences along with their accompanying emotions and affects form a residual substratum. In a kind of feedback system, new experiences tend to be organized according to the pre-existing pattern. The process is somewhat like ski trails: the first tracks of the day are reinforced by subsequent skiers, and it is finally very difficult to deviate and start a new set of tracks. Like ski trails, archetypes are traces of crystallized experience that constellate new experience and engage us in the search for correspondence in the environment.

Today some of Jung's theories have acquired more credibility in the light of studies of the persistence of memory in human DNA and in human cells, as well as from the evidence of morphogenetic fields and holographic theory. Some of the archetypes he identified, however, have been roundly criticized, particularly the archetypes of *anima* and *animus*. In Jung's view, the terms "animus" and "anima" referred to an unconscious contrasexual element—the anima being the feminine component of the male psyche and the animus the masculine component of the female psyche—in the male and female personalities.

Unfortunately, the concepts were rather lopsided. The anima-concept was full of affect, emotion, and many other feminine-identified qualities, and the animus was seen as a critical, negative, and aggressive inner voice. Demaris Wehr describes these culture-bound, gender-linked archetypes as "inner representatives of socially sanctioned, seductive but oppressive roles and behavior patterns."[5] Thus the animus is in reality a reflection of the culture's derogatory view of women's motives, intentions, and self-expressions, especially the assertive ones. The anima in men seems to work primarily by seduction and fantasy-projection. Most Jungians omit from their considerations of archetypes the ubiquity of patriarchy as well as misogyny, and the dialectical relationship between the individual and society. Thus Jung can be accused of ontologizing a socially constructed reality, and the numinous resonance of his notion of the archetypes seems to give a kind of divine sanction to psychological experiences that are culturally based. So there has been a certain reification of this "psychology" of women and of men.

It is also important to consider the subjectivity that gave birth to a dualistic, archetypal division. A recent German study of Jung, largely based on unpublished letters and interviews, proposes a disturbing hypothesis. In her book *Die Hiobsbotschaft C. G. Jungs: Folgen sexuellen Missbrauchs*,[6] Renate Höfer suggests that Jung's childhood experience of sexual abuse by a friend of his father left his consciousness "split," wounded by a traumatic dissociation that later imprinted not only his psychological theory but also his relations with women and even his political views. What she describes is a well-documented phenomenon in incest victims and might explain why Jung felt so alienated from the feminine in himself and why he was so ambivalent toward women.

On the one hand, the differentiation between anima and animus can unfortunately lend legitimation to culturally induced neurotic behaviors. On the other hand, as Wehr notes, it is a useful distinction in any effort to interpret the inner world of the enculturated Western male, with all of its fears, ambivalence, and repression. And I believe, analogously, it explains a great deal about civilization since the dawn of patriarchy, the Enlightenment, and technological culture. The anima of civilization itself, the *soul* of the culture, has been driven underground. The constellation of value that is associated with *masculinity*—that which is rational, logical, preferred, normative, serious, and privileged with power—is the visible and most-valued dimension of culture. And the constellation of value that is associated with *femininity*—that which is deemed emotional, carnal, natural, deviant or non-normative, not-preferred, trivial, vulnerable, and powerless—is the invisible, denigrated, repressed, and oppressed dimension of the culture.

In almost all the languages of the world, if one wants to express a "put-down," or denigrate something or someone, there is a veritable catalog of feminizing epithets to choose from. Whatever we devalue is usually feminized: racial or ethnic minorities, homosexuals, those who promote nonviolence. Social research also indicates that we learn our behavior toward devalued groups and minorities by practicing on women, usually from a very early age. Recent evidence of second-grade boys harassing little girls shows how early this begins.

Luce Irigaray, the French feminist philosopher, has speculated that what we mean by the "unconscious" is actually a "historically censored femaleness,"[7] a reality that women as well as men must repress in our civilization. Consequently, the culture itself denies and represses the real feminine and deals with it only in terms of caricature, through demonized versions or ideal abstractions. In a culture where the anima is suppressed, the dominators become amnesiacs. In her essay on lies, Adrienne Rich observes, "The liar [the denier] often suffers from amnesia. Amnesia is the silence of the unconscious. The stories women have been told about themselves are lies. But the liar is not aware of the lie. It is the repressed part of himself."[8]

The dynamism of these internal archetypes should not be underestimated. They are, indeed, often the unseen vectors of behavior. In much the same way that the anima complex can be an expression of masculine fear of the feminine and fear of loss of control in the liberation of eros, so the animus complex in women can be seen as the inheritance of an underclass. Ann and Barry Ulanov note the importance of the women's movement in this respect:

> The women's movement can be understood at least in part as raising to conscious challenge reductive anima images. The experience of so many women in so many cultures of a negative animus voice, persistent in its blaming, always declaring her efforts are "not

enough," "do not matter," "cannot succeed," can be understood as resulting in a massive internalization, over centuries, of an institutionalized misogyny.[9]

Turning from the micropsychological level and the inward experience of archetype to the macrosociopolitical dimension of experience, we can see the significance of the extraordinary coincidence of the rise of the women's movement and the turn "eastward" in the 1960s. Many pilgrims, worn out and depleted by the spiritual bankruptcy, materialism, consumerism, and sensualism of the West, went running to the East in hope of finding inner harmony, clarity, and spiritual freedom. They went to India, Tibet, and other locations in the Far East, seeking out the most ancient sources of wisdom and disciplines that could heal their unsatisfied souls.

In many ways it was a phenomenon much like the medieval pilgrimages to the Holy Land, when Christians traveled east to encounter the heartland of their faith. This was the era of the great cathedrals, all of which were built facing the east, toward the Holy Land and the Rising Sun of Christ. Unfortunately many of these pilgrimages were converted into Crusades, campaigns of slaughter, rape, and pillage of peoples who stood in the way of the West's notions of its own superiority and claim to domination. Similarly, at the same time that burnt-out, spiritually depleted Westerners were rushing to the Orient in search of wisdom, other Westerners were engaged in the crusade to dominate Southeast Asia, to hold Vietnam under Western hegemony.

This eastward phenomenon continues today. The osmosis of Eastern spiritual disciplines and philosophy has become a welcome antidote for the overrationalized dogma, noisiness, and materialism of the West. What is the meaning of this drift eastward? No other culture in the history of the world has been as "churchified" as the American culture. Denominations, congregations, cults multiply in this hothouse of religious belonging. But all the fellowship, all the devotions, all the rituals, all the dogma have left us starving for something more fundamental—the experience of the spiritual journey itself. Too much of what we identify as religious has been the effect of socialization. We are starved for something that will help us unlock and tap the wisdom and spirituality that we sense lie deep within ourselves.

The drift eastward is an epiphenomenon. An even more-transforming phenomenon is underway. The most universal and consequential spiritual movement in the world today is the movement toward self-valuation and self-determination among women. In every culture we find women, sometimes at great cost to their safety and peace of mind, questioning the prevailing forms of power—including religious traditions—all invented by the male culture and a masculine constellation of values, all modeled on dominance and dependency arrangements. The stirring, the questioning is universal. I believe that what is happening in women symbolizes and prefigures the destiny of the entire human community. It is the leading edge of the human agenda. The transformation that is in progress is in a larger sense the recovery of, the befriending of, the valuing of the feminine, the repressed anima of creation, a kind of metaphor for those values, those experiences, those people, those aspects of ourselves that this civilization has disempowered, denigrated, or lost. Some would say we are trying to recover our lost *soul.*

We are witnessing what the philosopher Foucault described as the prime catalyst of evolution: *an insurrection of subjugated knowledges.* I was reminded of the truth of this recently when I was reading a book by Orlando Patterson on the development of freedom in Western civilization. In his book *Freedom* he attributes the first stirrings of ideas of personal freedom in the Western world to women. He claims that Greek men were sensitized to the meaning of personal freedom by the complaints of Trojan women who were enslaved as captives of war, or by Greek women who lost status because of it. The impact of their experience and their presentation of pain—their subjugated knowledge—is part of our historic inheritance as a free people.

Certainly the Judaeo-Christian civilization owes its liberation to questioning, complaining, even disobedient women. Without the Hebrew midwives, Moses' sister and Pharaoh's daughter, without this courageous and determined alliance of women, there would never have been a Moses or an Exodus.

Today we are seeing the rising up of the subjugated knowledges of the outsiders of history—the undervalued, the oppressed, the outcasts, the disenfranchised; indigenous people, people of color, gays and lesbians, people who are differently abled, refugees, and above all, women. The wisdom, the knowledge, the struggles, the skills, the gifts of those who have been devalued are precisely what is needed to find our way to a sustainable future in a world of scarce resources, shrinking space, and radical differences.

The largest single group in the world now in the process of change is women. They have unleashed a hermeneutic of suspicion upon the entire mythology of civilization. In every corner of the globe, they are challenging, questioning, ripping away the curtain from the Great Lie, preparing the way for a new culture. Women have been the primary consumers and clients, subordinates and support staff for a patriarchal culture. Now they are becoming agents and subjects of their own history. Women are the largest single group who have had a lived experience that is reality-centered, "non-normative" for the dominant culture, and they are now beginning to own, name, and articulate that experience in their own terms.

What is the subjugated knowledge that women can teach the world? Back in the mists of primordial time, when they were still in animal skins, huddled around a communal fire, nursing and protecting their young, guiding and teaching them, walking miles to procure water each morning; inventing new forms of agriculture, studying and preserving plant life as a source of healing medicines, searching out and sharing scarce provisions, moving across new frontiers, solving the challenges of each day; finding a way to survive even when they were weaker than their male peers and enemies, when they supported each other with emotional closeness through the entire life cycle—when women lived like this for thousands of years, they learned things that no one else knows as well.

Women learned better than most of their male peers that you either share or you self-destruct. And because they were not power-

ful enough to create change by force or by edict, they mastered arts
of negotiation in resolving conflict, skills of cooperation, co-
responsibility, caretaking, and compromise. These human arts
have taught women how to survive through solidarity and cooperation rather than antagonism and competition. This is the wisdom
that the world has need of now. But how long will women remain
the carriers of this subjugated knowledge? As they are increasingly
socialized and integrated into the power structures of the masculine dominant culture, that question becomes more insistent.

This universal movement among women is a catalyst for change,
but there are those that fear change more than death. Thus the phenomenon of radical fundamentalism and the "rage of the right"
and "white male backlash" are predictable. Nevertheless, we seem
to be on the threshold of an irreversible historical shift. Patriarchal
culture gave us technology and modernity. Democracy gave us
equality—for empowered males. Capitalism gave us a way of orga-
nizing and accumulating resources—for the few. If we are to transcend the limitations of all three of these inventions, we have great
need of all the subjugated knowledges. The alternative is apoca-
lypse.

Somalia provides a grim paradigm on the contemporary scene.
In its painful history we see a microcosm of the past and very possibly our future, unless we can recover some of the subjugated
knowledges. In Somalia, as elsewhere, the struggle for gendered
power produces a dualism that favors patriarchal, technologized,
macho values. Somalians are fiercely clannish. And it is the mothers
who transmit the father's heritage to their children; children are
expected to memorize the names of perhaps twenty generations or
more of paternal ancestors. The clan structure rests on another
divisive reality: the division between the cultivators and the herdsmen. There are, or were, two cultures in Somalia. The cultivators
were settled, agrarian people, who created sustainable families and
communities, which they maintained in relative peace and harmony with each other as well as with animals and the environment.
Women were the central stabilizers in these communities. Historically the enemies of the cultivators were the nomadic roaming

bands of herdsmen who despised the cultivators as inferior, meek, and unmanly. They characteristically defined their own identity by feminizing the cultivators.

This balance of tension might have gone on for another century if it had not been for the introduction of Western technology. The introduction of trucks and guns into Somalia transformed the nomadic bands of herdsmen from a nuisance into a violent scourge. They ravaged the countryside, pillaged the stores of the cultivators, took possession of food supplies, accumulated animals, declared their dominance with an arsenal of guns, and used their new-found gains to buy more weapons and drugs. The roaming gangs are made up mostly of men and young boys. One twelve-year-old boy captured by the news cameras wore a T-shirt with "I am the BOSS" emblazoned across his chest. Famine, scarcity, and demoralization are byproducts of the destruction of a value system that was associated with women and children, harmony with nature, protection and replenishment of natural resources.

Reminiscent, isn't it, of the eighteenth- and nineteenth-century Americas when the introduction of guns, the horse, and liquor fueled the holocaust of indigenous peoples? Most of the tribal organization and way of life that we obliterated was based on the same values, strongly associated with women and nature, often under the patronage and power of women. The early settlers and explorers denigrated them as "petticoat governments." Today, in our inner cities we see the familiar scenarios and props of the social cancer: guns, autos, drugs, and roaming gangs.

Where do we look for signs of the emerging "subjugated knowledge"? How do we recognize the first strains of a new key, a new understanding of the human experience? How can we rescue this knowledge and apply it to our future and the future of the earth? As with the complaining women of ancient Greece, the "other voice" usually emerges first from pain. At first it is personal pain, stories of individuals who are able to put their experience into words or some other form of art or expression that communicates with immediacy. These precursors awaken others who have a similar shared reality, and soon there is a new "class" of people articulating their experience, one that departs from the normative in some way, an "alternative" experience. The emerging "other voice" describes a lived reality that is different from that of the dominant culture or the expected norm.

This pattern has been characteristic of the literature of subcultures in the United States, the fiction, poetry, and nonfiction that expresses and records the lived reality of being black in America, or Native American, of being a woman, or being gay or lesbian, of being Hispanic or Asian-American. These experiences generate new ways of looking at the social order, at history and politics, at institutions, at psychology and art, at philosophy and ethics, even new ways of looking at the self, at God, and at religious belief.

Feminists were among the first to challenge the androcentric bias of every aspect of the social and intellectual order, and a new feminist hermeneutic complemented racial and class deconstruction. Today the growing visibility of lesbian and gay culture and the new immigrants have accelerated the expanding universe of subjugated knowledges. The literature of *difference* is often the first harbinger of major shifts in social arrangements and models of power.

Japan offers an example of this same phenomenon, but in a very different social context. The other voice has only gradually been revealed in Japanese culture, perhaps due to a certain native xenophobia. When I visited the Peace Memorial at Hiroshima I was struck by the pathos of a sculpture of a mother carrying her child through the devastation of the aftermath of the A-bomb. It was a symbolic representation of the thousands of Korean and Philippine workers who had been enslaved by the Japanese during the war, many of whom were also killed or maimed by the blast. I learned that this part of the memorial was added only much later, after the awareness of the suffering of these people began to penetrate the consciousness of the Japanese.

The process by which the other voice is heard and recognized seems to resemble a familiar pattern of learning: the theory of cognitive dissonance. At first, the consciousness is deaf and blind to the new information. One cannot hear, for example, the pain and anguish of the experience that is different. Then, as awareness dawns, the other voice, the new information is heard, but only with irritation, with resistance or resentment. Finally, in the third stage of awareness, the other voice is recognized and heard with at least a beginning of empathy. The subjugated knowledge penetrates the consciousness and can be internalized.

In Japan, the "other face" of the feminine has been visible, but frozen in time. Some might describe it as a caricature. The external culture of Japan concretizes a certain feminine ethos and masculine values, anima and animus, in a kind of stylized tableau. The worlds of men and women are so separate, their obligations and expectations so different, that it produces a kind of harmony of rigid complementarity. Very seldom does one find visible expressions of female resentment or envy of male dominance and privilege in the public sector. It is as if the internalized myths of the personality mirror the social order; roles are so fixed and rigid that the limitation and the pain are hardly noticed or even experienced—until the mounting deaths of Japanese men from *karoshi* (overwork) or some other phenomenon sends a signal that stability does not necessarily indicate that all is in balance.

In contrast, in the United States the separate constellations of masculine and feminine values are internalized, whereas the external structures of society recognize only the masculine way. This sets up enormous conflict between women's inner experience of reality and the preferred cultural values. Homogenized America abhors separate-but-equal arrangements. Disharmony and friction, instability of sorts, is the price we pay for equality. Thus, we might expect that the divorce rate among Americans would be much higher than in Japan—the difference between the combination of fluidity and aspiration on the one hand, and fixity and acceptance on the other.

But Japan, too, is beginning to hear the whispers of a *subjugated knowledge*. One of the most significant sources of new literature is the emerging fiction of "the other woman." Stories that come from the experience of the "invisible" women of Japan—mistresses and, especially, the other woman who is also a single parent, the woman who must work—are beginning to awaken the consciousness and erode the monolithic view of the social roles of men and women. Stories by writers like Yuko Tsushima and Tomioka Taeko challenge the expected character profile and role behavior of typical Japanese fiction. Up to now the only images in literature have been the stories of long-suffering wives, domineering mothers, and prostitutes.

Another timely indication of the emergence of a new *subjugated knowledge* is the fact that in 1995 the Nobel Prize for fiction was awarded to Kenzaburo Oe, whose most notable work, *A Personal Matter*, is his memoir of being the parent of an abnormal, mentally handicapped child. The extraordinary story is a chronicle of personal anguish, shame, and a secret burden made visible and transformed into a source of insight, compassion, and creative energy.

One of my most memorable experiences of hearing the "other voice" was a recent art exhibition at my university, where several regional artists collaborated with several persons affected with AIDS to produce some remarkable works of art. My favorite was a panel-mural showing a series of pages from the Bible and superimposed over it were excerpts from the journal of a young man who has AIDS. It was stunning. Titled "Sacred People, Holy Words," it was the most graphic representation of the "other voice" as "revelation," unveiling—in the true sense of the word—a living reality that transcends old notions of how men and women and the world "should be." And I was reminded of Mark Thompson's insight, that "Gay men and lesbians possess the ability to lead society's next phase of cultural revolution—liberation of the soul—if only they realize that potential."[10] Gay men, so often "feminized" by the dominant culture, and lesbians, denigrated as "witches" by many, are among the messengers of the awakening anima of creation.

But another voice is becoming more insistent with each passing moment. And that is the voice of Earth itself, the source of life, the planet that sustains all life forms. Up to now, we have heard only whispers, and they were easy to ignore. Today the messages from the environment, from climate changes, from the whole ecology —

plants, trees, insects, frogs, viruses, the human body—are loud and clear. Mother Earth will fight back to preserve balance, especially against species that are a danger to the survival of life. Humans are now a self-endangered species.

The hills, the music,
White moon
Dripping silver over the trees
Mirroring
Your original face.

Ship of stones
Lost children
Mothers nurse them
For eternity.

Hirgana, Kanji
Katakana.
Listen for the light
To change.
Blind.

Chapter Two

God and Self:
The One and the Many

Nara was the first city that gave me a partial glimpse of the reality of Japan, the first mirror in which I saw clearly my own "difference." Nara was the first permanent capital of Japan, established in 710 C.E. A few decades later the capital was transferred to Kyoto. Both cities are filled with ghosts of Japan's origins and its past. Most of all, they are filled with gods and goddesses.

A day or two after my arrival I visited the Todai-ji Temple. It was a special day, when Japanese were honoring the great priest-prince Shotoku, who had done so much to establish Buddhism in Japan. Crowds filled the plaza in front of the temple; thousands lined up to take respectful turns purifying themselves with water and casting incense on the fire at the entrance. I felt caught up in a ritual that transcended mere tourism. I was aware that the temple was the largest wooden building in the world and that it housed the Daibutsu, the Great Buddha. When I actually entered the Hall of the Great Buddha, I was overwhelmed. Its overpowering presence, reaching more than sixteen meters above, consumed my senses momentarily. As a Catholic I have been surrounded by statues and effigies most of my life. I had seen St. Peter's Basilica with its gigantic forms, but there everything was to scale and one's awareness of actual size suspended.

Here, in front of the Daibutsu, one could only be aware of immensity and of imperturbable serenity. I suddenly felt puny and inconsequential, merged with something intensely *different*. At the same time I felt challenged, and yet totally accepted. I saw and sensed the oceanic compassion that Buddha has come to represent. Neither the Buddha nor I could speak, but I knew somehow that an important conversation had begun.

A few days later I had another stunning encounter with the Buddha. This time it was in the ancient city of Kyoto at the Sanjusangen-do Temple. The name of the temple means a "hall with 33 spaces," a long, narrow building which houses 1,001 statues of Kannon-Bosatsu, the Buddhist god/goddess of mercy. When I entered the great hall, an endless regiment of Buddha-like figures confronted me. The gold images—life-size or larger—overwhelmed my perception with sheer multiplicity and infinity. Here was the perfect symbolic representation of the fundamental Buddhist tenet that Buddha has many incarnations. The huge Kannon at the center had eleven faces and forty ("a thousand") arms. On either side there were five hundred more statues that repeated the image—each with slight, hardly noticeable variations. Each arm of "mercy" is believed to save twenty-five worlds. Whenever I saw Japanese praying, it was often before an image of Kannon, much as Catholics pray very visibly to the Virgin Mary in her many shrines. With the conventional three handclaps, then a reverent bow, the Japanese cling to their own traditional image of a compassionate mother, a powerful incarnation of the Buddha.

Images of Kannon are everywhere in Japan. Like the Buddhas they are curiously androgynous in their appearance; sometimes the guidebooks refer to the image with the masculine pronoun, but more frequently with the feminine. This aspect of blurred gender intrigued me, and I eventually pursued the origin of this fascinating icon. In a later chapter I will say more in regard to this figure.

Although Buddhism did not have its origin in Japan, its enculturation there has embedded it very profoundly in the Japanese character. D. T. Suzuki, the famed philosopher of Zen, believed that, although imported from China and ultimately India, Buddhism found its most fertile soil and expression in the Japanese culture.[1] In many ways it represents the Eastern consciousness, just as the Judaeo-Christian tradition defines much that is Western. In the

East, Buddha waits for every Christian, Muslim, and Jew with a question. Since returning from Japan the encounter and the dialog begun there assume more significance for me every day.

One of my most memorable encounters in Japan was the opportunity to visit and dialog with the Buddhist priest-teacher-psychologist and author Rev. Shun'ei Tagawa, chief abbot of the Kofukuji Temple in Nara, the "home" temple of Yuishiki Buddhism.[2] Two others who participated in the dialog were my faithful translator-companions, Paul McGrath, a reader of several books I have published, and Keiko Morita, a reader of several books by Tagawa. We spent several hours at the temple monastery and enjoyed a very stimulating discussion.

Tagawa's familiarity with psychology in Japan and the United States made our encounter doubly rich. My own background in the study of religion, theology, and myth complemented my training in clinical psychology, so we found many points of mutual interest. In my first book, *Kiss Sleeping Beauty Good-Bye*, I constructed a three-phase paradigm of spiritual-psychological development which we discovered bears some similarity to the stages of spiritual development that Mr. Tagawa has illuminated in his teaching and writing.

Tagawa is a practitioner and teacher of Yuishiki Buddhism of the Hossoshu sect, perhaps the most ancient and strict sect of Buddhism. He explained that this was a Buddhism that placed supreme importance on the imagination, in contrast to Zen. My own interest in myth and Jung's concept of the collective unconscious connected with Tagawa's *arayashiki*, or "storehouse of the unconscious." Keiko noted how science, astrology, and alchemy seem to have been running parallel for a long time and now seem to be converging.

The conversation focused for a while on the concept of "image." Tagawa believes that every action plants an imaginative "seed" in the unconscious. I noted the correspondence of this idea to the Jungian concept of archetype, a kind of patterned potential for energy. Meditation is the art of identifying and connecting with these images. Our contact with these images is significantly

blocked, according to Tagawa, by media and the amount of information pouring through the top of the consciousness. He believes
this contemporary condition has made it virtually impossible for us
truly to meditate. We lose track of the self because of the flooding
of information—we must learn how to limit it. The *arayashiki* is the
plane of real existence; if we are not connected with it through
"right action," we are dissatisfied. This dissatisfaction can persist
after death.

At this point in our conversation, "reincarnation" surfaced in
everyone's mind. Tagawa's view of reincarnation was distinctly different from some of the popular views of our time. If the flesh per-
ishes and the dissatisfaction persists, reincarnation takes place
because the soul is still attached to life. When there is a sense of
things left undone or problems unresolved, one cannot achieve the
freedom of the final enlightenment. I asked Tagawa about
Dzogchen, the Tibetan Buddhist idea that is the basis of the
Tibetan Book of Living and Dying. Clearly Tagawa's Buddhism
interprets the afterlife in a relative sense. As he put it, "If a person
succeeds in attaining enlightenment—in becoming a Buddha—
reincarnation stops there."

But he sees the similarity between Dzogchen Buddhism and the
effort of the living to procure the best possible reincarnation for
the dying or deceased. Here we remarked about the parallels
between the "49 Days" of Dzogchen, and the Christian memorials
of the dead at seven, thirty, and fifty days following death. These rituals seem to transcend cultures and predate the great religious
traditions.

Tagawa was interested in the research I had done on God-
images. The purpose of my study was to design an instrument to
examine the character of God-images and how they correlated
with a measure of mental health.[3] While I did not intend to analyze
cultural differences in these images of God, nevertheless the
sample was large enough so that some interesting differences
emerged. Among Asian residents or Asian Americans in the
sample, the notions of God—if they existed—were vaguely polytheistic, even animistic. They contrasted significantly with the more

Western conceptions of the Euro-American subjects. The Westerners' images were well defined and monotheistic, for the most part driven by abstraction. The question arose in my mind: Are the Western notions of God an "artificial implant" in contrast to the Eastern Yuishiki belief that God-images originate in human action?

I commented that the West, driven by the Logos, eventually superimposed Protestantism on the Judaeo-Christian tradition. Early Christianity was much closer to the Image and to Eros. Catholicism retained some of this in its rituals and devotions to saints. Many of these images and rituals were rooted in a more ancient mythic system connected with the Terra Mater and the image of the Earth as female. Protestantism, on the other hand, organized society around ideas and doctrines and the power of the Word; Logos was preferred to Eros. The more ancient images have been driven underground, but they still exist in the collective unconscious. The question arises, Can we retrieve these buried images now to help people move forward psychologically to a new perspective—of the world and of the self?

After a brief discussion of the *Seven Works of Vasubandu,* a series of poems that summarize Yuishiki Buddhism, I asked Mr. Tagawa if there was a specific discipline that had to be practiced in order to reach this spiritual consciousness. He replied that, since it is so linked to the *arayashiki* or "unconscious," it is virtually beyond our understanding and control. Hence the proper posture is not a "management" of oneself, but a passive receptivity—or so it seemed to some of us. Paul and I, the two Americans in the dialog, had discussed the spiritual passivity of Japan on a previous occasion and were simultaneously wondering if this might have a connection with Buddhism. Mr. Tagawa disagreed. "That's hardly the case. In Buddhism the individual is engaged in the positive process of 'seed-sowing' through one's choices and actions."[4]

As we talked more about these spiritual "seeds" that plant images in the soul, I wondered if there might be some common elements in the *arayashiki* and in the idea of a collective unconscious. Tagawa said yes, but that there were also elements that were unique and specific to the individual person. "These are the seeds of what we will do tomorrow. We are making our tomorrows as we act. It's not as if these 'seeds' exist somewhere to be picked up: what we are really talking about is energy."

After several hours of discussion, we proceeded to a nearby tea-house for a luncheon, Japanese style. The positions that I found so uncomfortable for eating were natural to our Japanese hosts. As I savored and thoroughly enjoyed almost everything that was served, I noticed that our priest-monk took only a very small amount of the food that was served and with his customary, emotionally reticent demeanor.

At one point in the discussion, Tagawa said that the goal of Buddhism was to *be rid of preference*. In many ways he was a visible icon of this aspiration. The dualism that we struggle with in the Western tradition, the distinctions between mind and body, beauty and ugliness, superior and inferior, good and evil, wealth and poverty, life and death—all become the criteria for "preference" and the source of so much of our unhappiness. Tagawa put it in very simple terms: "Think of the human preference for beauty and our reluctance to accept the ugly. We clear a path for beauty, making sure that the ugly keeps its distance. This energy contributes to the activation of vanity in the individual—so the whole thing has to go, in Buddhism." As I was to discover later in our correspondence, this is precisely the spiritual core of the moral philosophy of Kannon, as he describes it in his book, *Kannon Bukkyo No Kokoro* (*The Heart of Kannon Buddhism*).[5]

Later that night when I was alone in my hotel room, writing notes in a journal, I suddenly understood why the dualisms of the West made an *insurrection of subjugated knowledges* so necessary. To what extent had these social preferences been produced, legitimated, reinforced by the Judaeo-Christian-Islamic traditions? Was any religious tradition, any human condition, East or West, free of such preferential dualisms?

All of the great religious traditions embody legitimated wisdom that has been enculturated in specific ways in particular times and places. Spiritually each tradition harbors an anima, a repressed, rejected "other," a subjugated wisdom that functions very much like Jung's *shadow*. The spiritual pilgrim must inevitably confront, acknowledge, and integrate this shadow, or remain incomplete. So the Christian, Jew, and Muslim must meet and dialog with the Buddha and the questions that the Eastern traditions pose for the West.

When one visits another culture for a short period of time, one can take away only impressions. But even impressions can reveal something about the authentic character of a people. Japan's spirituality has often been described as an amalgam—of Shintoism, Buddhism, and Confucianism—and of the many "new religions" that have proliferated in the post–World War II era. Nevertheless, I came away from my Japanese sojourn with the distinct impression that Japanese spirituality is grounded in Shinto, and in an indigenous, even aboriginal, consciousness that was its predecessor. These roots have been somewhat obscured by the Japanese reluctance to show allegiance to a mythology that for so long was associated with the imperial dynasty and emperor worship. But regardless of how individual Japanese feel about the Shinto heritage, its imprint on Japanese consciousness is everywhere.

In contrast to Christian theology and Christology, the Shinto tradition might be said to have a "kamiology." *Kami* refers to something that is sacred or possesses divinity. It can signify heavenly gods or earthly spirits that dwell in shrines and guardian spirits; it can also refer to special persons, departed ancestors, and all kinds of natural phenomena such as trees, boulders, waterfalls, mountains, rivers, birds, and animals. It includes everything that is extraordinary, highly virtuous, or worthy of awe.

Shinto emphasizes this immanence of divinity in creation, and especially the intimacy, the closeness, between kami and human beings. Kami are omnipresent and acknowledged openly. The primitive animism has evolved into a kind of "polytheism," although there has never been a distinct native concept of God or a supreme being among the Japanese. Shinto is defined as *kami no michi*, "the way of life according to kami." One observer notes,

> The Japanese notion of kami is so different from the doctrine of God in Judaism and Christianity that it is helpful for Westerners to

keep in mind the contrast between the two. In the Judeo-Christian tradition, the formal teaching about God emphasizes the transcendent character of the one and only true deity (more than the immanent presence of God within the world and human life). Generally, in both Judaism and Christianity, the relationship between a human being and God involves a formal act of faith, an acknowledgement of the existence of God and a conscious decision to accept God and live in obedience to him. By contrast, kami are many, and although they may hover above the earth, they are also within the forces of nature and within the lives of people. Kami are considered to be everywhere, and traditionally, the Japanese assume the presence of kami as naturally as they see beauty and fertility in nature—no conscious act of faith is needed.[6]

In Japan I saw the spirituality of Shinto subtly woven into the texture of Japanese life—from the stunning torii gateways to the magnificent temples, from the family rituals to personal attitudes, through myth and memory; life is lived with a different perspective.

The monotheistic consciousness of the West leaves little room for the relativism of the East. Monotheism necessitated exclusion: of other gods, of ideas that did not conform to a standard, of people who did not fit a definition. Monotheism literally created a single myth-based symbol system for the West and a philosophy of history. It legitimated binary logic and fostered the production of abstract rather than imagistic thought, necessitated strict definitions of right and wrong. It abhorred ambiguity and plurality. The One God was above all, before all, the origin and end of all that exists, the rationale for all human activity. Modern Islamic fundamentalism is perhaps the best example of this radical monotheistic consciousness carried to the limits of its logic.

Nothing so reveals the difference between the Japanese/Eastern consciousness and the Western consciousness as our respective views of and relationship to nature. Historically the Japanese have regarded nature as permeated with kami, with divinity. "In Japan, God, as creator, is absent, and therefore, human beings seek comfort by attempting to immerse themselves completely in nature."[7] Contemporary scholars believe that the unique relationship of the

Japanese to nature may be rooted in the imaginative consciousness of the aboriginal people of the islands, the Ainu and their ancestors. As with indigenous people of many lands, the Ainu, the *emishi,* have been subjugated and purged for centuries. Still, something of their consciousness survives in their oppressors, the dominant culture of Japan.

Art focuses on nature and illuminates it, praises it in lyrical, worshipful modalities. In the Judaeo-Christian tradition, nature is the creation of God and completely subject to the will of God. Nature is reduced to an object. The message of Genesis is clear: man, as God's deputy, is to rule and control nature. We have been given "permission" to use it up, because it is "lower" in the abstract hierarchy of being that God established.

When the British scaled the world's highest peak, Mount Everest, the event was recorded in the West as "the conquest of Everest." Huston Smith notes that when the Japanese team scaled Anapurna, the second highest peak, they climbed to within fifty feet of the summit and deliberately stopped, as if out of respect for the mountain's sublimity.[8] Thus in Japanese psychology, the goal of the relationship with nature is *communion*. In the Western world, the goal is *stewardship* or *conquest*. To the transitory visitor, however, it is clear that in practice this difference is being blurred increasingly by Japan's uncritical, unbridled adoption of a capitalistic economy, which inevitably plunders nature. I saw evidence of this not only in the news reports of Japanese corporate behavior, but also in the habits of Japanese consumers. Nature is honored symbolically, but not always in business practices or in personal lifestyle.

The psychologies of East and West are deeply rooted in the myths surrounding the two great mountains, Fuji and Sinai. The two mountains are symbolic of the locus and ethos of divinity and spiritual energy, East and West: Mount Fuji, the majestic *axis mundi*, is the place where the cosmos and the kami, heaven and earth, intermingle and radiate outward. Mount Sinai, a mountain that God chose as the place where a covenant, a code of right and wrong, an exclusive way, would be established with a particular, "chosen,"

people. The covenant of Mount Sinai produced a society of righteousness, of law and judgment, and consequently a potential for
intensified divisions, adversarial tendencies, and adherence to absolutes. Fuji, on the other hand, signified the sacred womb of creation where the harmony of the primal pair-gods gave birth to life.

When Prince Shotoku wrote the first constitution for Japan, the
most important value was harmony or *Wa*, the right relationship of
all things and the avoidance of adversarial or oppositional behavior.
More importantly, the principle of *Wa* rejects absolutism. Buddhism found a ready soil in Japan and reinforced the inclusive
aspect of Shinto with its teaching that the universe and everything in
it are expressions of the one, eternal Dharma. Ultimately there are
no distinctions between particular objects. All is One, One is all.[9]

In contrast to Judaeo-Christian societies, the concepts of individual sin and private guilt find little resonance among Japanese. As
the ancient teacher-leader Shotoku asks, "How can anyone lay
down a rule by which to distinguish right from wrong?"[10] On the
other hand, the West is firmly grounded in negative theology, a
powerful superego, and what psychologist Karen Horney has
called "the tyranny of shoulds and should nots." My own observations in Japan confirmed my experience as a therapist with many
Asians: they experience very little personal guilt for deviating from
abstract prohibitions or principles, but suffer a profound sense of
social shame for offending the spirit of *Wa*, or disappointing or dis-
connecting from their family. Theologian Koyama sees in the spirituality of Mount Fuji and of Mount Sinai the contrast between a
cosmological and an eschatological consciousness:

> If the world of nature-oriented religions produces "instant gods,"
> then the world that speaks of the "maker of heaven and earth" often
> takes "the name of God in vain." When the name of God is taken in
> vain, the scourge of idolatrous tyranny will eventually visit human-
> ity. . . . This is a destructive "theological" operation. Often the failure
> of eschatological religion brings more dread upon humanity than
> the activity of people dedicated to the cosmological instant gods.[11]

The nontheistic kamiology of the Japanese and the syncretistic
tendency of the culture permits them to take advantage of many

wisdoms, if they choose. It is not uncommon for Japanese to be ini-
tiated in a Shinto ceremony as a child, married in a Christian ceremony, follow Confucian principles in public life, and after death,
he or she will most certainly be buried and mourned according to
Buddhist rituals. Many Japanese homes contain both a kami altar
and a buddha altar, and the Japanese language contains a word to
include all of the "divine" manifestations: *shinbutsu*, "gods and
buddhas."

My encounter with the pantheism, polytheism, and relativism of
the Japanese consciousness challenged my Western perspective.
Never before had I seen so clearly the consequences, for good or
ill, of the monotheistic consciousness. Nietzsche warned that the
idea of a normative God, "beside whom there are only false, spuri-
ous Gods," was a consequence of a belief in a normative human
being—and thus legitimated all sorts of bias, prejudice, imperi-
alisms, and tyranny. A contemporary observer notes:

> In Western culture the polytheistic theology that would enable us to
> "name" our plurality . . . died with the collapse of the Greek culture.
> From then on our explanation systems, whether theological, socio-
> logical, political, historical, philosophical have in the main been
> monotheistic. That is, they have been operating according to fixed
> concepts and categories which were controlled by a logic that
> demanded a rigorous and decisive "either/or": either true or false,
> either this or that, either beautiful or ugly, either good or evil.[12]

These bipolar moral and political extremes still motivate our
social order today. Indeed the monotheistic consciousness has
organized our thinking in very efficient ways, and it has produced
an individual that is superbly endowed for competition and the
"survival of the fittest." The Western *self* is made in the image of the
Western God, and this was another challenge with which Japan
and the East confronted me.

In the ancient world, body, consciousness, and soul were con-
ceived as a continuum. But as the psyche mimicked the epistemology of monotheism and monism, it contracted into an "ego," a
solid self. The primordial consciousness, which was more oceanic
and symbiotic, experienced the self or the "within" as a "shifting

flow of subjective feeling," not at all equivalent to the modern sense of personal agency and inwardness.

Changes occurred in the quality of consciousness over time as cultures passed from oral to literate phases. Recorded memories intensified individuation, as did migrations, the impact of pluralism, and the loss of boundaries. The transition is documented in linguistic history. In their modern connotation, the words for "individual" and "self" emerge as late as the Middle Ages in their modern connotation. With Descartes, Locke, and the associationists, the self was disengaged from embodiment, mechanized, reified, and atomized. The rise of positivism completed the transition: the self as "body/soul" vanished. In 1943 Allport claimed that positivism had reduced the self and the soul to "ego." Berman has compared this encapsulated, individualized ego to the ultimate product of the scientific revolution, the uranium pile.[13]

The Western acceptance of the material as the boundary of the real reinforced the notion of the independent, disconnected self. And the monotheistic consciousness added the assumption, and the necessity, of *omnipotence*. Lacan once described the Western ego as a paranoid construct, founded on the logic of opposition and identity of self and other: a logic that requires boundaries.[14]

I have elaborated on the rise of the "imperial ego" in the American culture in another book, *Lost in the Land of Oz* (New York: Crossroad, 1991). Americans, perhaps more than any other people, do not see themselves as continuous with their environment, do not see their reality as a "given," and do not readily see themselves as part of a larger interpersonal context. Thus, the ego (the solidified self) crystallizes as a result of the overwhelming impact of reality.

In Japan I was struck by the theism and nontheism of our respective Western and Eastern cultures, and its relationship to the conception of the self and to social expectations. We talked many times about the differences between Japanese women and American women, which seem more obvious than the differences between the men, perhaps because Japan's male culture is so inebriated with Westernized workaholism. Japanese women admire

American women, but many of them believe that it is impossible to achieve the "American woman's dream" of being a professional, a good mother, wife, and publicly active person in one life. The Japanese woman is more likely to accept trade-offs and construct a workable balance among these roles. Dr. Iwao of Kansai Women's University speculates on this lack of "perfectionist attitude" among Japanese women:

> Perhaps it has something to do with the culture's religious beliefs: If human beings instinctively seek to make themselves resemble as much as possible the ideal represented by the god or gods they worship in their culture, then in societies with a mono-theistic, Judeo-Christian tradition, that ideal is of the omnipotent individual. In the case of Japan, where ancient indigenous animism, Buddhism, and Confucianism are part of the religious culture, the realm of the divine is divided up among innumerable deities (so that different shrines must be visited to pray, for example, for success in love or in academic achievement or in job hunting). In this culture [Japan] no one god is expected to take care of everything, and human beings are likewise thought, as a matter of course, to have unique strengths and weaknesses. Those very individual weaknesses are what makes it necessary for people to help each other and to cooperate; they provide the basis of interdependence and equality in a human society built on division of labor. Perhaps the ideal of the individual as the all-knowing and all-powerful god precludes the recognition of the need for division of labor.[15]

Dr. Iwao suggests that, in societies with the monotheistic bent toward abstract principle, people may be coerced toward conflict and distorted behavior, when the path to a goal is "not necessarily linear but one that winds and twists along the way." Thus the Western concept of individualism is a mirror image of the transcendent, omnipotent God.

The Eastern view of the self rises from very different roots. The Chinese word *jen* captures one aspect of this view. The central focus of the concept of *jen* is the place of the individual in a web of interpersonal relationships. Desires and goals, as well as anxieties, are judged according to whether they contribute to or erode the individual's personal relationships. The Eastern perspective sees the person as an integral, inseparable part of a larger and more important whole; whereas the Western view sees the person as the center of everything.

The Japanese perception of the self is another variation on the Asian theme, for it is based on the essential unity of the *iemoto* and the *ie*. These terms refer to the master–disciple relationship and to the household. There is very little horizontal mobility in the Japanese culture, and the dependency relationships of kinship organize the private and public world. Relationships of pseudokinship are extended to the corporations and other institutions. This identification with kinship structures is valued over individual uniqueness and autonomy. Thus the Asian self is a more permeable and changeable entity, because the need for belonging and being in harmony is as important as the need for food, air, water, and space.[16]

The issue of "space" is directly related to the way our cultures deal with conflict and tension. In a dinner conversation I was asked to name something that I did not understand about the culture. After a moment's thought I said, "Sumo. What explains the fascination with a phenomenon that appears to be less of a sport than a display of deliberate overeating and conspicuous girth?" My questioner replied by tracing the Sumo tradition to the era when small people needed visas to pass through a warlord's territory, but larger people did not. Sumo is about command of space, and the larger you are the more likely you are to have an advantage in terms of power.

This led to an extended discussion of the effect of "space" on the Japanese and American character. Japan has always had insufficient space for its population. North America has always had surplus space. Japan, with one-twenty-fifth of our land mass—much of it uninhabitable—has one-fourth the size of our population. Historically the struggle for space and the necessity of living crowded together has generated certain adaptations. Of necessity, rules of decorum and emotional control are embedded in Japanese behavior.

One of the most difficult things that a Westerner may encounter in the Japanese is this stoicism and reticence. Feelings are guarded as very private, and emotional reactions to many situations or experiences are visibly muted. The Noh theatrical mask is the perfect analog for the Japanese way of communicating by concealing. Traditionally there has been a clear distinction between expression or appearance, *omote*, and intention or mind, *ura*. *Omote-muki* refers to that which is public, open, official; *ura-muki* suggests something private, closed, personal.[17] These two values run like the warp and woof through all of Japanese life and seem literally to structure the consciousness. Japanese know they cannot speak about everything they are thinking, and it is often impossible to know by their words and gestures what they are actually thinking and feeling.[18]

These behaviors are extremely functional adaptations for promoting *Wa,* or social harmony, and reducing conflict. But as some observers have noted, the result may be an excessive prudence and reticence that verges over into deception. Psychologically, this split in the self can also plant seeds for despair and suicide, particularly when Japanese are increasingly confronted with Western cultures and values that do not dissemble so deliberately. Americans, in particular, are the polar opposites: open, assertive, relatively unself-conscious, not so attentive to verbal or contextual cues in the public presentation of the self. The Japanese range of appropriateness is much narrower, and the range of emotional transparency very limited.

This became apparent to me when, a couple of times, I forgot this difference and asked my Japanese hosts for a personal feeling response about something. What would have been a typical, non-threatening, bland query in the United States was decidedly intrusive and inappropriate in the Japanese context. A few weeks later, after the earthquake in Kobe, I was reminded again of the stoic reticence and denial of self-importance as I watched the TV cameras searching in vain for dramatic personal narratives from the Japanese survivors.

In the weeks that followed I saw news reports about Kobe's "second agony," the inability to deal with the overwhelming effects of the trauma of the earthquake. As Western trauma counselors offered their services, everyone wondered whether these techniques would work in a society where emotions and pain are repressed and psychological treatment is still shunned. Recent local reports indicate that, as Vietnam did for the United States, the tragedy of Kobe may help to diminish the taboo against psychological treatment and increase access for all Japanese to mental-health services.

A surplus of space has certainly given North Americans the luxury of saying exactly what is on our mind. So has the horizontal egalitarianism of our social relations, which allows more elbow room and a higher tolerance of directness and open confrontation. The spatial differences between our cultures are psychological as well as physical. The spatial, expansive dispersal of the North American culture and the more fluid kinship ties can also leave some individuals isolated and terribly alone.

Unquestionably as a therapist I have faced different challenges in dealing with the "solid self" of the Western personality and the more "permeable" self of the Asian personality. Many of these differences are clearer to me since my visit to Japan. To give them some coherence it is necessary, as I have attempted here, to begin with the primary religious consciousness. In psychology today we use a term called "primary background object" to suggest a fundamental, archetypal element in the consciousness that organizes the personality. Similarly, this primal force organizes the culture as the dominant ethos and engine of history. In the West this engine has been the Judaeo-Christian myth, a monotheistic belief in an omnipotent being. In the East there is no parallel because the cultures are for the most part nontheistic or polytheistic.

This basic difference in background orientation produces two different psychologies, two models of consciousness. In the West the dualism engendered by monotheism drives the culture toward rationalism and the primacy of abstract principle but makes it vulnerable to literal mindedness and either/or exclusionary thinking. The polytheistic consciousness and belief in kami that characterizes Japan produces a healthy "relativity" and inclusiveness that exalts the importance of feelings and relations. But this disposition clearly has limits, and into the archetypal void (where there is no primary background object) flows the *group* and the kind of monocultic loyalty that it possesses in the Japanese consciousness. The weaknesses that result are only too obvious: a pronounced xenophobia and hostility to outsiders, and a vulnerability to the strong paternalistic or cultic leader. Japan's recent experience with the Aum Shinrikyo cult and the terrorism it generated are testimony to that vulnerability.

And what of the sources of Western moral vulnerability? Instead of a monocultic society that exalts group identity, we have a polymorphous society that spawns "omnipotent, autonomous egos." There is much in this fact to explain why our society is vulnerable to disconnected anarchists like Lee Harvey Oswald (John F. Kennedy's assassin) and Timothy McVeigh (the alleged Oklahoma bomber) or the Unabomber, as well as to paranoid paramilitary groups, supremacists, and other outlaws. And, we too have seen how vulnerable to cultic gurus a rootless, mobile population can be in the absence of strong kinship ties.

The Japanese self is fluid because it bears the imperative of allegiance to the group and of adhering to appropriate role behavior. The Western self (in democratic societies) bears the burden of creating a self. Undoubtedly many of our would-be assassins and terrorists are seekers of celebrity, which literally gives them a publicly verified "self." The isolation and envy of many of our dysfunctional personalities illuminate the pathology of our culture, just as the conformity, dissembling, and repressed hostility illustrate the pathology of the Japanese culture. "Separation," especially from the primary parent (usually the mother), is seen in our culture as a necessity for mature development. Sometimes it is the price of admission for success or a good job. It can mean dislocation from roots or the loss of a marriage. Americans have grown used to this kind of mobility, necessitated by our freedom and autonomy. In the Japanese culture the primary social value is in the preservation of "non-separation," and thus the necessity of loyalty to kinship structures, of social reserve and harmonious courtesy.

The Judaeo-Christian myth underlying our culture reinforces the

necessity of separation by predicating our relation to a monotheistic, omnipotent God on the radical separation inherent in the
"fall from grace," the alienation from divinity recorded in Genesis.
The Western experience of existential angst, anxiety, and longing
has been associated with this primordial myth and all the implications of a belief in original sin.[19] Ethical norms as well as guilt—in
the Western consciousness—are experienced in relation to adherence to, or deviation from, the absolutes that are inherent in a
monotheistic, encapsulated reality modeled after a unitary,
omnipotent power. In contrast the Japanese ethic is situational,
and guilt or personal shame is experienced in relation to failure to
meet social role expectations.

Understanding this difference has helped me to understand why
some of my Asian clients have demonstrated an obsessive need to
conform to social expectations and to preserve dependency relations but show a decided lack of personal accountability for some
behaviors. In the Anglo culture, guilt often seems to fixate on the
"inferior" functions, particularly sexuality, which the mind/body
split has devalued and demonized. The mechanism of guilt is
directly related to the difference between the superego of the West,
which exalts the "I," and that of the East, which exalts the "We."

Asian attitudes toward the physical, material world tend to be
fluid. On the one hand there is a residual animistic feeling that
nature is inhabited with kami. On the other hand, there is also a
belief that the material world represents unreality, that is, it is un-
important or even an illusion. Hence, the Eastern tendency is to
take passively the world as it is, accepting its vicissitudes without
struggling to change it. The Western consciousness, however,
equates the material world with reality and enters into a kind of
combat with it on two fronts: striving for self-creation or personal
conversion and actively working for transformation of the social
order. The peculiar mix of religion and politics in the United
States, where democratic atomism flourishes, is a case in point. It is
fertile ground for crusades of all kinds.

Rituals often capture the essence of a myth and a tradition. They
are at the heart of the Judaeo-Christian tradition. The myth of Exo-

dus has been a historical catalyst for change; this story of deliverance and liberation has inspired many other revolutions in the history of the world, from the French Revolution and women's suffrage to the black civil rights movement of the 1960s. If we look carefully at the ritual enactment in the Passover meal, we see a paradigm or template for relating to the world. I call it the *solidarity of blood*.

The Israelites are facing extinction; they are ready to flee. These Israelites achieve their identity and cohesion through the shedding of blood in circumcision. The meal must include the shedding of blood, the sacrifice of an animal. The doorposts must be sprinkled with blood, which will give identity and protection when the angel of death passes over. The people are to eat the meal "with your loins girt, sandals on your feet, your staff in hand." They cannot be at ease; they must be prepared, armed for the journey. "You shall eat like those in flight."

They are to eat everything. Anything that remains must be burned. Perhaps this is why they were instructed to eat unleavened bread—"dead bread"—which has no other principle of life in it that can survive this holocaust. Nothing shall remain to seduce the people back into exile. The Passover meal ritualizes the deliverance of Exodus, but it offers a paradigm based on the *solidarity of blood* as exclusive and imperative. It is a unity that we have seen over and over again in the history of the modern world: a unity based on race, or class, or nationalism, or religion, or craft, or cult, or some other shared interest.

In the New Testament parallel, we see a variation on the paradigm. Table fellowship was a distinctive mark of Jesus' ministry and the Last Supper was both a celebration of his ministry and a farewell. This time the blood of the Passover is symbolic of the sacrifice he will make. The supper is a *koinonia,* a sharing, a communion, a *solidarity of love*. The new covenant of love, in the Christian view, provides a new basis for kinship that goes beyond the solidarity of blood. This new covenant is inclusive; even those who don't have a "wedding garment," a title to membership, are welcome. The new covenant of love is nonhierarchical; no one is valued more than any other one. Jesus promotes a new discipleship of equals: when his followers argue over who is the greatest, he acts out a parable of humility, "I am among you as one who serves." And "so shall you be each other's servants."

The price of unity is sharing: the disciples on the way to Emmaus do not recognize their fellow traveller until they break bread with him. In the ancient Passover paradigm, we must recognize and know the other as no-stranger; then come the unity and sharing. In the New Testament Passover, we must first love, even a stranger, and share our substance in order to achieve recognition and unity.

Both of these paradigms have organized Western civilization in a thousand ways. They are deeply embedded in our spirituality, and they are part of the warp and woof of our social order. In Japan I discovered the Tea Ceremony and was struck by the way it expressed the core values of a distinctly Eastern spirituality.

In Nagoya, Japan, I visited a very historic Tea House where I was introduced to the Tea Ceremony. I accepted the invitation of my guide, expecting to find and witness a very stylized ritual. I found, instead, a way of life; I participated in a timeless moment, a feeling of being in absolute harmony and balance with the entire universe. The traditional Tea House is regarded as a house of peace. The gift of tea makes it a place of nourishment as well as healing. The formality is a form of moral geometry intended to inspire mutual respect, harmony, purity, and tranquility. Small objects as well as small gestures are extremely important. The room is usually empty. The light filters through the paper screens, and no corner of the tatami mat is in darkness. Only the tea stand, perhaps one scroll on the wall, and a simple flower in a vase can be added. Simplicity, starkness, and beauty. Everything is designed to discourage superfluity and symmetry, which is regarded as repetition.

Everything is designed to respect and honor nature. The construction of the Tea House or Room is a harmony of natural materials, all of which suggest temporariness, fugitiveness. The traditional Tea Room usually accommodates no more than five persons. All are welcome: the commoner, the samurai, the lord, the stranger. Nonviolence and the adversarial spirit must be left at the door; traditionally all arms and signs of rank were removed before entering. The guest dons a traditional *yukata*, a simple housecoat made of unobtrusive colors. The ritual symbolizes and models communion with the inner essence of all things and immerses one in the experience of harmony and balance. It is very representative of a spiritual discipline, a subjugated knowledge, that complements Western wisdom and Western ways. In the kingdom of tea there is no room for excess, for addiction, for rampant consumption, for obscene accumulation of power or things.[20]

As Westerners, there is much we can learn from the spiritual disciplines and ritual myths of Asia. Likewise, I believe the East has something to learn from the spirit of Jewish Passover and Christian "Agape"—the dynamics of exodus from oppression, the fidelity to justice, the transforming love that promotes solidarity and social transformation.

When I arrived in Japan, the Buddha met me with a question. I expected the question to be, "Who is your God?" That was not the question. Raimundo Panikkar has illuminated my own experience:

> What matters, then, is not "God," in the classic sense. What matters is only a path, a way that leads in the direction of liberation. Ultimately our lot is in our own hands. We and we alone can deliver ourselves from the suffering that assaults us on every side. . . . One need only rely on the Buddha, who has indicated the way, and on the community—that is, on solidarity. The Buddha has not affirmed God, but neither has he denied God. On the contrary, as we have seen, he defended himself against the latter accusation even more earnestly than against the former. But he is unconcerned whether or not we satisfy our speculative quest.

Panikkar notes that the fear inspired by an all-powerful, transcendent God often drives human beings to the opposite extreme: making a god out of the self. Instead, he says, the Buddha proposes a third way that delivers us from both false projections. "Hence the sense of liberty in the message of the Buddha."[21]

I returned from Japan and my "journey into difference" with new eyes and sharper insights. I understood more clearly what it is that makes me Western and discovered some of the things that characterize the Eastern consciousness. I returned with many seeds that were planted in my conscious mind by teachers like Buddha and Lao Tzu and Tagawa. And I found new ways to understand the seeds of the unconscious. I gained many new perspectives on nature and the self, on sin and guilt, the monotheistic psychology of the West and the polymorphous psychology of the East. I see new connections between space and emotions, and how the value of *Wa* weighs against the value of righteousness. In a very short time I learned a great deal about *difference* and explored a whole new continent in the geography of my soul.

Now, at home again, I find myself looking for signs of convergence, of the blurring of opposites, the mellowing and mingling of ethos and ethic, the early shoots of mutuality and universality. In Japan I had seen the rise of new literatures, particularly in the voices of forgotten women. From many Asian countries we have heard the echoes of a new revelation, the wisdom literature of suffering and of patient struggle for a great reversal. It is the same voice coming from all Third- and Fourth-World peoples, whether it is the Korean *han* or the liberation theology *de base* in Latin America. The new sounds are those of weakness turned into strength and of inclusiveness burning away class distinctions, of *difference* as the leading edge of the future.

Even in the traditional theologies of the West, the undiscovered and unhallowed experience of the past is being mined for precious wisdom. Creation spirituality and the mysticism of the Beguines and other holy women are displacing the sense of the Fall with Original Blessing. And it is especially in spiritual movements like ecofeminism that the variegated strands of conscious and unconscious giftedness are emerging. Symbolized and actualized in the belief systems of East and West, this double helix of strands of difference, interwoven in a new social "genome," has the potential to birth a new social order.

Many years ago, Carl Jung offered a prescient insight. Although he was reflecting on his own experience he might have been prophesying the destiny of the human community.

Growing acquaintance with the spiritual East should be no more to us than the symbolical expression of the fact that we are entering into connection with the elements in ourselves which are still strange to us.[22]

Temples
Serene and dark.
To know not possible.
Follow flying carp.

> *Wisdom.*
> *Juice of the grape*
> *Ripens slowly on the vine*
> *Then bursts.*

> *Woman of Japan*
> *Speaks no word*
> *But flashes in the sun*
> *Dragonfly.*

Chapter Three

Gender Masks and the Third Sex

We live in an era of disappearing boundaries. The drive toward self-determination and freedom, toward self-enhancement, is natural to our species and irreversible. Since the 1950s many boundaries have dissolved or become more permeable: sexual mores, political barriers like the Berlin Wall and the Iron Curtain, trade barriers, travel barriers. Boundaries and borders are more accessible also because of the technology of communication and transportation. But the cost of these new freedoms is greater vulnerability. The mobility and the aspirations of whole populations, the velocity of capital, the massive increase in pollution and environmental deterioration, and the instability of a global economy make us all endangered passengers on the planet.

Biologically and psychologically, the disappearance of borders and shifting populations have made us more vulnerable than we realize. No threat remains regional, local, and limited for very long. Everything that can circulate does, whether it is ideas on the Internet or viruses in the blood. Encounters with *difference* are guaranteed. Neither our minds nor our feelings, much less our immune systems, will be spared in this tidal wave of exposure. Freedom generates choices, and choices generate *difference*.

Like the other myths and expectations that encrust the geography of our soul, gender and sexuality are a prime source of social as well as psychological conflict in our times. As a therapist I find it is one of the most problematic areas that affects mental health. The blurring of boundaries has impacted on how we think about *gender*, by which is meant expectations and behaviors connected with a social role as man or woman; and *sexuality*, by which is meant the individual's sense of self as a sexual being, one's preferred expression of sexuality, orientation, and object choice.

I was very curious to see what the Japanese experience would reveal about *gender* and *sexuality*. My impressions began from the moment I left the United States on a fourteen-hour flight to Osaka. The plane was crowded with businessmen, but also with families and children. I was struck with the way the Japanese mothers treated their male toddlers. These mothers were extremely indulgent with their little sons, sometimes exceeding the tolerance of the other passengers. The little boys (when not required to be in a seat belt) could express themselves freely, in loud voices or shrieks, walk or climb over whatever they pleased, do what they wanted with their food. Their whims and pranks were indulged with absolute patience, and they were continually enfolded in maternal embraces and reassurances.

I was amazed, having expected to find Japanese children well behaved and deferential in their social relations. On the other hand, the little girls of the same age seemed to have been "programmed" already to behaving well; they were relatively quiet, unobtrusive in making their wants known, very attentive to adult behavior. One little Japanese girl did get cranky and act up—she definitely did not receive the same indulgence as her male peers on the plane. I stored this impression in my mind to test on future observations.

A week later another revealing vignette was added to my collection. This time it was a group of adult Japanese males, from all appearances, work fellows who were on holiday—sans women and children—at a Japanese temple-museum in Nara. The group was careening through the museum, loud and boisterous, heedless of others in their path, careless in knocking into some of the exhibits. They were obscenely drunk, and to my amazement, the security people more or less ignored them. It was hazardous to get in their way and seemingly indecorous to notice the condition they were in. One behavioral characteristic stands out: I noticed that two of the men who were not so drunk acted as "nannies" for the others, directing them, making sure they did not misstep, even holding them up on several occasions. The general nurturant embracing among them struck me as a contrast to the stoic, taciturn Japanese businessmen that I observed on the street or in the train stations.

I was also unprepared for the hordes of schoolchildren and teenagers that I encountered every evening in the train stations. The sea of youngsters converged on the transportation depots daily in the late afternoon. As far as the eye could see, there were hundreds, thousands, of Japanese students, all in uniform, looking as if they had just marched out of an old-time Catholic parochial school—girls all clumped together in one part of the station, boys in the other. The contrast with dismissal behavior in a typical American public school was dramatic and amusing. This was something of a surprise, by contrast with the United States, where adolescent boys and girls mingle so casually, where dress codes are only moderately successful in coping with outrageous costumes.

Later, after closer acquaintance with the Japanese society and its norms, I could interpret my impressions. Having observed the rigid separation of male and female worlds, I learned more about the powerful role of the mother and the absent husband and father. I discovered that Japanese women are little concerned with identity and most concerned with their role. They indulge male children up to the time when they enter school; then they become their harsh mistresses, pushing and pressuring them through an educational system that prepares them for university entrance exams but does little to promote critical thinking or creative curiosity and imagination. Sometimes these young people I saw in the train stations at 5 P.M. were on their way to a second school for evening classes, usually referred to as *juku*, where they would spend more hours in intensive drills guaranteed to prepare them for the exams.

Women are so deeply committed to this role of preparing their children for "success" that a not-so-complimentary epithet has been coined for them: *kyoiku mama*s or "education mamas." As a psychologist I wondered about the effect, particularly on the males, of this apparent shift in the mother's role from one extreme to another. The high rate of adolescent suicide in Japan suggested one answer. Another answer was visible in the drunken men on business holiday at the museum.

Japanese admit they have a problem with alcoholism and ritual drinking among the "salarymen." Because it is tolerated and "expected" behavior for loyal officemates, few health or medical practitioners in Japan deal with excessive drinking as a condition to be cured. Thus, according to one report, the incidence of liver disease and alcohol-related problems is high in young men in their thirties. The enforced workaholism and long hours in the workplace provide another inducement to substance abuse as a relief.

But I also cannot forget the overindulged little Japanese boys on my flight to the Orient. There is research that connects alcoholism with early and developmental deprivation of touching and other forms of nurturant behavior. I wonder, in retrospect, if the drunken men who were embracing and holding each other, regressing like children, were not struggling to recover a maternal nurturance that was suddenly and painfully removed when they entered school. Perhaps this maternal "wound" is also the explanation for the role that the mistress and prostitute play in the life of many Japanese males.

In any event, these impressions and speculations are merely footnotes to an overall observation that cannot be denied: up to this point in history, the worlds of the two sexes in Japan have been radically separate. In Japanese society the pressures for this polarization and asymmetry are enormous. Singleness is still seen as an abnormal state. No one wants to be single; yet no one expects marriage to bring happiness.

Here the contrast with American expectations is dramatic. A 1990 survey, which Iwao records in her book *The Japanese Woman*, reveals startling differences between American and Japanese women's expectations. For example, among younger Japanese women only 35 percent consider fidelity of the spouse important. Among American women across all age groups 85 percent consider it important. Likewise, issues like good communication, a good sexual relationship, and feeling "in love" are far more important to American women than to most Japanese women. Thus the reason for the huge differential between the Japanese and the American divorce rates becomes painfully obvious.[1]

Will these differences remain indigenous to Japanese society?

There are clearly many advantages to the way things have been. Many Japanese women believe their way of "separate spheres" is the best way to preserve their independence as women. In fact most Japanese married women have total control of their household and children, of the family finances, more control over their time than their husbands have, and the freedom to do things in their "preferred way." They are not eager to take on the conflictual "double burden" that is so familiar to the American working mother, wife, and companion. Moreover, there is still widespread belief that the differences between men and women are innate and that their respective needs are best served by the traditional territorial divisions.

But the winds of change are already being felt. Many men no longer want to run the risk of being a candidate for *karoshi* and premature death. In one of the hotel magazines I noticed an article on "the new Japanese man," who cares as much for his family as for his company. Young women are more interested in career skills. Surveys indicate that younger Japanese women are also more concerned about finding a man who can be a true companion, who can communicate with his spouse and participate in parenting. They want to feel "in love" with the man they marry. These new values are surfacing as younger women begin to participate in the corporate economy with greater frequency. As early as 1971 pioneer feminists were saying it was not a question of being angry with men: "What I want is not a man or a child, I want to have a stronger soul with which I can burn myself out either in heartlessness or tenderness. Yes, I want a stronger soul."[2] This is an eloquent statement of the aspiration of the contemporary woman for herself, as well as for her partner.

Current statistics provide another thermometer of change. According to a recent government survey 25 percent of young single Japanese women have no intention of marrying, compared to 14 percent in 1972.[3] Perhaps the most obvious indication of the growing breach in the wall between the sexes is the emergence of the "other woman" and the "single mother" from invisibility, and the more recent increasing visibility of the gay phenomenon in Japanese society.

In a time of "boundary change," what happens when *sexuality*—that is, sexual desires and behavior—no longer conform to the social expectations associated with *gender*? This is a question that surfaces constantly in my practice as a therapist. Young people are fearful and confused and curious about "alternative sexualities." Parents are anxious and alarmed: "What if one of my children should . . . ?" Middle-aged partners are panicked, anticipating the dissolution of their marriage if they should reveal their sexual orientation. Single men and women are suspect if they are differently oriented, or if they remain celibate too long. My experience of these struggles in the United States context made me curious about Japan.

While in Japan I had two conversations that illuminated the situation of women and men whose sexual orientation sets them apart from the expected norm. Both conversations, one with a young Japanese woman in her early twenties and the other with a young Japanese man in his late twenties, could have taken place in the United States, where many young adults seek the privacy of a therapist's office to talk about their struggles with *difference*, within themselves and within society. I learned from my conversations in Japan that the struggles are very similar, but socially at a much earlier stage, and intensified by the more rigid expectations of conformity to social role. As in other cases of perceived *difference*, persons who are consciously and publicly lesbian or gay in Japan are treated as if they have an imported disease, one of the consequences of Japan's predilection for consuming American products and life-styles.

In Japan Yin and Yang are so crystallized in the social order and so relegated to clearly demarcated sexual territories that there is little room for visible deviance. Among certain social classes in the United States, the concepts of *masculine* and *feminine* no longer convey deterministic, exclusive categories, but rather denote clusters of qualities that are not necessarily "natural" to one sex or the other. This leaves room for variation and creates a certain space—albeit full of risk—for people to come out of the closet. Japanese have no word or phrase in their language to describe such a situation. So people who wish to live their truth visibly in society, especially if they are young, run a gamut of rejection, denial, pathologizing, and demonizing, and, worst of all, disconnection and invisibility. Even if they do find a supportive community of friends, their existence is often reduced to "passing" in a society that marginates or denies *difference* to an even greater degree than in the United States culture (at least this was my impression).

Historically, as in most societies, homosexuality has always existed in the Japanese culture. For centuries, many undoubtedly have lived submerged in the surrounding society, invisible and often isolated. However, in the East, as in the West, people of different sexual identification and/or orientation sometimes found "safe houses," more or less institutionalized communities where they could be themselves, where they would be safe from "compulsory heterosexism."

In the West the clerical and religious traditions of all faiths provided such havens from ancient times. In the East, particularly in the Buddhist tradition, there were analogous institutions. The monastic tradition was grounded on celibacy, which for all practical purposes signified more of a same-sex identification and distancing from the opposite sex than it did strict abstinence. The lives of Buddhist nuns, which only recently have been a focus of attention among Western historians, reveal strong parallels with the development and structure of Western religious communities of women.[4] As in the West, the pressure to conform to the social role of marrying and bearing children was heaviest on women. Thus the development of women-centered enclaves was a strategically countercultural choice, ostensibly devoted to the pursuit of spiritual goals, but also providing an option to social role expectations.

In the early Western church, widows, deaconesses, and canonesses often lived communally in secular situations. In time these communities evolved into more structured monastic institutions. Male hegemony in Christian society and the need to have women under control left women with two options: the old canonical principle required them to be *aut maro, aut muro,* that is, underneath a man or behind a wall. At least up to the Protestant Reformation, Christian women had one way of avoiding cultural pressures to marry: entrance into a religious community or monastery of women. Most of these were nevertheless supervised by patriarchal and often misogynist churchmen, but day-to-day life freed these women from the vicissitudes and coercion that marked most women's domestic lives, and left them free to pursue education, creative arts, and spirituality.

One alternative life-style was so popular that it actually became a threat to church authorities, who finally colluded with local governments to eliminate it. These were the *beguines*. When the larger monastic orders no longer had room for all the women seeking entry, and when middle-class women began to have the same aspirations for safety, freedom, and the association of women, beguinages and beginenhofs sprouted across Northern Europe from 1100 to the late 1300s. The beguines organized themselves around their need for free expression of feeling and spirituality, their desire for companionship of women, and their preference for a simple life-style and self-sufficiency in work.

Scattered at first, the clusters of women gradually took on more of the qualities of community and enjoyed incredible growth. By the year 1260 there were 8 houses of beguines in Cologne; by 1320 there were 97 houses in the same city. By the middle of the thirteenth century a Dominican historian calculated there were over 2,000 beguines in the city of Nivelles, and 600 in the city of Strasbourg. In 1317, one historian estimates there were 200,000 beguines in Germany alone. Sadly this option for women was ruthlessly cancelled by churchmen, who saw these "loose women" as a threat to their authority. Between the papal bull of 1311 and the ensuing Inquisition, beguines were virtually purged from Europe.[5]

All that survives of this remarkable phenomenon are a few architectural constructions that dot the European landscape, a half-dozen old ladies in the Lowlands, and—remarkably—some of the most beautiful love poetry and mystical writing of the Western world. The life-style obviously liberated a creativity and spirituality that was the expression of Eros, an *embodied knowing* that was a stark contrast to the stoic dualism and predilection for Logos of the patriarchal culture.

As in the West, the Buddhist male monastic tradition forbade all contact with women, but seems to have been more tolerant of homosexual contact. The relations of monks and novices were rooted in the master–pupil relationship that permeates all dimensions of religion and culture in the East. Few distinctions were made between commerce of mind and body in these relations. Outside the monastery homosexual brothels near Buddhist temples proliferated in the Edo period in Japan. Homosexuality or love between men was extolled as the highest form of love, very much in the same tones as among the Greeks. Among the macho Samurai, homosexual encounters were the norm.[6]

Historically another safe haven where gender boundaries were blurred and homoerotic interests accepted, both East and West, can be found in the artistic and theatrical communities. Japan has two particular cultural expressions of this phenomenon, the Kabuki theater which involves only men (some of whom play women's parts) and the unique Takarazuka Young Girls Opera Company (some of whom play men's roles). The latter is an all-girl revue that is organized like a vestal virgin enclave. According to descriptive reports, virginal, righteous, and beautiful girls are chosen from the best families. They live a cloistered existence in Takarazuka. Their living situation is off-limits for men, and they are educated and groomed for their roles. The male roles in the productions are the most sought-after parts in the troupe. As in Kabuki, the theatrical transvestism serves an aesthetic purpose, but Westerners are typically baffled by the ardor that cross-dressing excites in predominantly straight, heterosexual men and women in the audience. Could this be an erotic release from the constriction of the socially expected gender roles?

Perhaps this highlights an underlying archetypal function that homosexuality performs in a culture. It may be the harbinger, the precursor, not only of sexual ambivalence but also of genuine social change. Levi-Strauss once noted that "Buddhism expresses a placid femininity which seems to have been freed from the battle of the sexes, a femininity which is also suggested by the temple priests whose shaven heads make them indistinguishable from the nuns, with whom they form a kind of *third sex*. . . . Buddhist sculpture often expresses a kind of androgyny, transcending the sexes."[7]

In Japan, social roles explicitly demand different behaviors of male and female genders; but in the domain of sexual fantasy, ambivalence seems more acceptable, and there is a wide spectrum of tolerance, less taboo and pathologizing. Homosexuality has, incidentally, never been treated as a criminal deviation or sickness.[8] In the West, particularly in the United States, it is just the reverse: greater tolerance for deviation in the social roles of the genders and less for *difference* in the expression of sexuality. Perhaps where gender roles are more rigid, homosexuality and cross-sex eroticism may be indulged as a fantasy, whereas in the United States the fluidity of gender roles makes everything possible in real life. Homophobia haunts us because of this fluidity.

So we can see the conflict about to emerge in Japan, China, and other Asian countries. As a culture it is approaching a "boundary crisis," a time when social pressure to breach the barrier between male and female roles is reaching a critical mass. This development is intrinsically linked to the political economy.

Patriarchal societies are based on the accumulation of power in the hands of a ruler or a selected few. They depend on a very clear demarcation of roles and a hierarchical distribution of morsels of power. Control of gender roles and sexual expression is implicit in these societies because labor as well as reproduction must be controlled. Today many cultures are in the process of emerging from these patriarchal structures. In terms of political economies, some have emerged since the time of the Enlightenment with the birth of a new awareness of the individual. In the post–Enlightenment period there was great interest and priority placed on abstract concepts of human rights. We moved from an era when "might equals right" to a new era when "right equals might." This coincided with the industrial revolution and the ensuing separation of the home from the workplace. A new, rational perspective and respect for "natural laws" constructed the political economy. Complementarity and respect for the innate differences between men and women created the necessary glue for social arrangements and a sustainable society. Power was distributed more downward, but it was still necessary to keep functions, sexes, social classes, and races separate but equal.

Today as the demand grows for something more than a rhetorical democracy, pluralism and capitalism provide the soil for dissolving the remaining artificial barriers, the membranes of power. In a society based on Darwinian capitalism, "possession equals might." Theoretically, power is accessible to all but goes to the "fittest," the one who has the advantage. The individual can now aspire to be anybody, to have anything. But individuals have to compete not only with other individuals but with new conglomerations of power: political, financial, corporate.

The psychology of capitalism impacts on everything, particularly sexuality. Ultimately it dissolves the divisions of role and consciousness that are necessary in other kinds of political economies. Now, everything is accessible and possible for both sexes, in terms of gender role, in terms of sexual expression. Complementarity in the family is replaced by symmetry; roles are interchangeable. The voices of fundamentalism throughout the world as well as our own homegrown neo-right decry these events as signs of degeneration. In reality they are simply signs that the forces of democratic capitalism, which seem inevitable in the developed and developing world, have burst the social membrane. We now have to learn how to live politically, economically, and psychologically in an expanding universe of pluralism. How we experience ourselves and express ourselves sexually is part of that universe.

So, cultures like China and Japan, who have imagined and tolerated only controlled forms of gender behavior and sexual expression, will have to learn—if they continue on their current economic trajectories—how to cope with increasingly individualized choices in every dimension of life. This lends credence to John D'Emilio's view that the "homosexual" category of personal identity only emerged with the free labor system—under capitalism.

> The expansion of capital and the spread of wage labor have effected a profound transformation in the structure and functions of the nuclear family, the ideology of family life, and the meaning of heterosexual relations. It is these changes in the family that are most directly linked to the appearance of a collective gay life. . . . Only when individuals began to make their living through wage labor, instead of as parts of an interdependent family unit, was it possible for homosexual desire to coalesce into a personal identity—an identity based on the ability to remain outside the heterosexual family and to construct a personal life based on attraction to one's sex.[9]

D'Emilio notes the great irony in the fact that capitalism, which has so enshrined the family and traditional values, actually undermines it. Theoretically a pluralism of sexualities is inevitable in a culture evolving toward a free economy. In this respect, the efforts of the Chinese government to exclude gay and lesbian groups and issues from the recent United Nations conference on women seem ludicrous, as the same government plunges headlong into an increasingly capitalist political economy.

In such a paradigm shift, gay men and women often become scapegoats for our discomfort. Rather than scapegoats they might better be regarded as accidental catalysts, or simply as reflectors of the increasing pluralization of society. In thinking about sexuality, Euro-Anglos are handicapped by the binary, dualistic, dichotomous strains in Western logic. So it is difficult to accept the fact that sexuality is, finally, a mystery, a conundrum. While there is a great deal of evidence for genetic dispositions that nurture a particular sexual orientation, there is also much evidence to suggest it is something beyond "the dance of the chromosomes." Sometimes we forget that, as a species, we are still evolving. Nature is not finished.

One perspective on the future of socialized sexuality is already mapped out in the developmental experience of the individual. In an insightful essay called "Sexual Autonomy as an Evolutionary Attainment," the author traces the development of the individual in sexual terms:

> The *core gender identity*, a psychological emergent, follows the principle of the early embryonic stages, i.e., with both masculine and feminine potentials at the start; but at this stage, with a critical period at around twenty months postnatally, a choice is made not with vestigiation but with dissociation of the unselected alternative. [John] Money stresses a correlation with linguistic attainment since the child's command of gender words will be crucial in determining what he assigns sexually to others and to himself. The attainment of language at about age two thus establishes a critical period for gender identity. After that period a reversal is hazardous to undertake since it is practically impossible to accomplish and the attempt may result in serious conflict and confusion of the sexual role. But

Money here leaves open the fate of both bilingualism and bisexuality. . . . The alternative is not destroyed. It remains latent in the personality as a possible form of sexual communication.[10]

The essay goes on to extrapolate from Money's view a paradigm of human development. Mature personality assumes a bipotentiality, a certain plasticity of masculine and feminine behavioral potentials. The author sees the development of the individual as a gradual unfolding of three gender phases: *ambisexual, disexual,* and *amphisexual.* The infant is ambisexual, neutral as to sex role. By the time of puberty the individual is usually clearly disexual; it demands the inhibition of the alternative gender behavior and divides the human into mutually exclusive genders. The third phase, amphisexual, is usually triggered by creative work or by parenthood. This phase expands with age. It is not a sense of being bisexual; it is a gradually acquired freedom, in varying degrees, from the "cultural lens," the "grid of definition," the *self as defined by gender.*[11]

Could this developmental pattern in the individual be analogous to a pattern of cultural evolution? Do highly developed cultures inevitably accelerate toward gender depolarization? Evidence suggests that this may be true. Anthropologically, humans are the most weakly dimorphic vertebrates in regard to male/female differences. Many other species show more exaggerated differences, both physiologically and behaviorally. Why nature required two sexes for reproduction has puzzled many scientists. Two sexes create relational conflicts; parthenogenesis would have been much more energy efficient. Altruism, a crucial requirement of genetic survival, is more likely when everyone is the same. Sociobiologists have suggested that the crucial reason for the existence of two sexes is that it promotes *diversity* in reproduction. In other words, through genetic recombination it shuffles the chemical constituents enough to insure health, hardiness, and survival.[12]

What happens to the human species as we take an extraordinary, even if gradual, leap from being a *reproductively* determined species to a *creatively* determined species? If anything characterizes the twentieth century it is precisely the onset of this new era in evolution. An infinitely expanding population cannot survive. Not only does personal freedom demand choice in regard to reproduction, but the survival of the species will demand creative innovation and intervention. To meet this challenge, some suggest that nature, the cosmos, and the evolving psychosocial order will provide a new kind of human being.

Psychologist Sandra Bem believes that the cultural lens—a compulsory heterosexism that enforces all sorts of dominance paradigms—has poisoned human relations. Heterosexism, not heterosexuality, eroticized all sorts of inequalities. Dualism, which split off sexuality from spirituality and amputated feeling from thinking, inevitably placed an exaggerated burden on sexuality. Gender relations and consciousness carry the weight of this distortion.

Bem proposes that a new kind of person—a "gender nonconformist"—is the future of the human species. Bem is not predicting or advocating a race of genderless androgynes. She is describing a consciousness in which homosexual and heterosexual are no longer mutually exclusive classes of persons, a consciousness that can include within itself the possibility of variations in object choice, in modalities of sex and love—at least for others. It is a consciousness that is no longer frightened by what it has repressed, and no longer denigrates what it does not choose or desire. Bem describes this new evolutionary consciousness:

> Included in this category are all of the people whose lives seriously violate the androcentric, gender polarizing, and biological essentialist definition of a real man or a real woman—all of the people, in other words, who would have been thought of as sexually inverted in the late nineteenth and early twentieth centuries: gay men, lesbians, bisexuals, transsexuals, transvestites, and "gender-disordered" children, who continued to be pathologized even after the concept of sexual inversion had gone out of fashion. Also included in the category are feminists, both male and female, who actively oppose the gender scripts of the culture, and even the relatively traditional men and women who become gender nonconformists merely by reversing some critical aspect of the male or female script—by choosing, if they are women, to sacrifice marriage and children for an ambitious full-time career, and by choosing, if they are men, to do the reverse.[13]

It should be added that other marginal persons seem to fit Bem's definition: certainly many celibates and a fair number of unmarried persons. In the beginning, in which we are presently engaged, these new humans will be seen as mutants and will be pathologized and demonized. They will endure all the paranoid and phobic reactions to be expected from a dominant culture. But gradually the *subjugated knowledge* and wisdom of this "otherized" consciousness will influence the future of social relations. Feminists, celibates, communitarians, gays, and lesbians—like the ancient monks, mystics, and solitaries— are paradoxically conservators of the culture as well as catalysts of change.

Down through the ages, some men and women have either lived this reality implicitly and/or conceptualized it explicitly. A *third sex* has been developing, like evolution, at a glacial pace. The solitary, the celibate, the midwife, the medicine man, the artist, the gay man, the lesbian, the single mother, the feminist are all transforming elements in the culture. To the extent that they mimic the dominant culture in hoarding power, displaying tribalism and exclusivism, indulging in irresponsible behavior, in misogyny or racism, exploiting or using others, then they become a social poison. In this respect gay persons can look like reverse mirror images of gender-bound personalities. This digressive narcissism might slow, but in the end it will not divert evolution. Gender nonconformists—whether homosexual, heterosexual, bisexual, or celibate—bring two particular gifts to the human community. First of all, as many psychologists and anthropologists have noted, this "otherized," devalued, outsider, subordinate role often gives a person exceptional *insight* into what is actually going on in the surrounding power structure. In the case of women and minorities, they have much more understanding of the dominant white male consciousness than vice versa.[14]

In the case of homosexuals they must live with a contradiction: their inner being says something is natural and right; society says it is wrong. To survive they must learn to trust their intuition, their *embodied knowledge*. Like all those who are gender nonconformists they develop a "third eye" that scans their social environment in a kind of continuous social analysis.The gifts of *insight* and *embodied knowledge* are a positive and sustaining contribution to the social order.

Modern civilization rests on a foundation of gender polarization; it is the primary carrier of value and power associated with male privilege. The gendered personality, like the gendered culture, has a predisposition to superimpose value classifications on every heterogeneous collection of human possibilities that occurs. Research shows that these classifications are biased and constitute the "glue" that holds dominance-dependency models in place. Moreover, it shows that conventionally gendered individuals are more likely to organize information in terms of gender. They are, for example, more likely to attribute (erroneously) statements made by women to men or assume that a praiseworthy project or work of art is the product of a masculine consciousness. They are more likely to trivialize what the "others" accomplish. They are more likely to avoid even minor activities that might be perceived as inappropriate for their sex. They literally see the world through the lens of heterosexism, and in that bias they devalue and disempower social arrangements and adaptations that might contribute more to a sustainable society and an evolutionary consciousness.[15]

Whatever their particular life-style, true "gender nonconformists" are the catalysts of the next phase of evolution. From them we will learn new ways of interpreting reality, new forms of kinship structures, new modes of generativity and creativity, new alternatives to moribund structures. From them can come a radical critique and transformation of the capitalistic political economy. One wonders if the clusters of single and/or gay yuppie consumers and careerists in our urban areas are aware of the challenge and the opportunity that may be passing them by.

Homophobia, from this perspective, is fear of the future—fear of living in a world of potentiality instead of a world of essentiality. When we bury any potentiality in our unconscious, we sow the seeds for spiritual disruption, conflict in the social order, and conflict in the self. Ann and Barry Ulanov cite the example of Adolph Eichmann, the efficient master administrator of Hitler's extermination policy in World War II. He is reported to have been disturbed by a compulsive attraction to Jewish girls.[16]

Certainly, there are collective parallels in the United States history of racial repression: our literature is saturated with insurgent black images and phobias in the white consciousness. An even more obvious example of a subjugated knowledge that was repressed and oppressed in the ages of the Inquisition is the case of women executed as witches. Any kind of embodied knowledge was a threat to the secular and church establishment. Women's knowledge of medicines and child-birth, of healing therapies, even their "familiarity" with animals was suspect. Women who were perceived to have a special knowledge of and relation to animals were often accused of being witches. If they were seen communicating with animals, it could be a death sentence. The dominant rationalized patriarchal consciousness could not admit or perhaps not even imagine the possibility that another species might have equal claims to attention, care, and affection.

What these diverse examples suggest, as we have noted in preceding chapters, is that any part of ourselves that is rejected becomes a reservoir of negativity that ultimately is projected outward. It is not only a psychological problem but inevitably a sociopolitical problem.

> The revenge of an unrecognized, unlived Self is persecutory feeling toward others, which finds its gleeful translation in scapegoating—racial, sexual, religious, economic, political, cultural, whatever or whoever lies at hand.[17]

So many of the *subjugated knowledges* buried in the Western unconscious seem to be manifestations of *embodied knowledge*. Women, who have preserved more of this kind of knowledge, therefore, become a pivotal element in negotiating what the future of the human species, and of all other species and life forms, will be. To be truly embodied and not cut off from one's body-soul is to be able to *feel with*, to empathize with other persons, species, and life forms. What will be the boundaries and priorities of human behavior in the world of the future? We will find the answer in the confrontation with *difference* — in our world, in our culture, in ourselves, even in our history. A great moral dialectic concerning how we shall live as a planetary culture has begun.

All one has to do is look at recent political shifts in the Western countries, especially the United States, to realize that the first arena for that debate is sexuality. Sexuality seems to be the nexus, the interface of what cultures have done not only with the *body* but with *feeling.* We will not be able to tolerate pluralism in the expression of sexual desire or know the limits of that expression until we have dissolved our alienation from the body, and the repression of feeling. Our sex-driven culture has blurred the meaning of Eros, suppressed its embodied knowledge, given it an aura of narcissism, and cut us off from other creatures and life forms. As our political and religious traditions cling to the ethic of repetition and reproduction, the subjugated knowledges that might shift us to a paradigm of creative intervention and conservation are silenced and seen as a moral threat.

Most of the developed cultures in the world have created special places for attempting to recover body/spirit integration; they are called, among other things, spas. I ended my visit to Japan with a two-day retreat at a hot spring *onsen*. I came to my brief retreat with an overload of new experiences that left me mentally exhausted, yet exhilarated by a new culture. The effect of sustained hyperalertness and stimulation was as expected: no time to process the new experience and thus, a "split" between the experiencing body and senses and the mind, which was starved for time to do its own experiencing. The time I spent at Oniwa Onsen restored the balance. The solitude, the presence of beautiful surroundings and walking trails, the Japanese interiors and traditional decorum, the authentic Japanese cuisine—full of so many delights, pleasing to the appetite and the eye—and the healing hot spring baths made me whole again. It was as if a giant magnet had gathered all the scattered filings of my being, and balance—unity—was restored.

The tourist and the occasional visitor encounter mostly the busy, instrumental, driven side of Japanese life. And I could fit the excesses into that portrait: the alcoholic binges, the compulsive educational system, even the "floating world" of women converted into commodities, the pornography, the cruelty and violence of many entertainments. All of these are a counterpoint, perhaps even antidote, to the essential social restraint of the people. But behind the paper screens of public decorum and the necessity of the social mask is a more traditional attitude expressed in the intimacy with the body.

At the hot spring or *onsen* one could catch glimpses of the ease with nudity, the attentiveness to sensual delights, the genuine effort made to spoil the guest with any pleasure required. In Japan, before the emphasis on Neo-Confucianism, and perhaps some degree of contamination with Christian scruples, the sexes were mixed in the baths and whole families pleasured themselves there on holidays.

The bath actually takes place before the dip into the volcanic hot spring. The ritual requires much soaping and rinsing in a room full of stools and buckets. One day a group of several women were bathing when I arrived. I enjoyed observing them out of the corner of my eye as I prepared myself for the hot spring. It was almost as if they had completely lost track of time. They soaped themselves and chatted, and washed each other's hair, and soaped the smaller girls and the oldest women in the group. It was like a ritual massage. I assumed they were an intergenerational family or kin, and marveled at the gentle, affectionate, and sensual ways they touched their own bodies and each other, without self-consciousness or shame. The entire ritual, almost like a dance in slow motion, with the polyphony of intimate talk, hypnotized me into the same rhythm. Weeks later I found an echo of my own experience in the memoir of another American in Japan:

> I'm fascinated by this ritual attention to the body, so different from the brisk Western morning wake-up shower. When I finish (again) and go to shampoo my hair, I see that most of the women in my group are still scrubbing. I give up. It must take practice. I have never seen such luxuriant pampering of bodies. . . . I have never seen people more comfortable with their bodies.[18]

On two other occasions I have spent a day at a German spa. Ostensibly the nudity and the ease with the body was there, but the ritual was very different. It was almost industrial in its sequence: from the pool to the sauna to the ice cold dip to the jacuzzi to the shower, then begin the cycle again. The massage was as vigorous as the ritual. Men and women were not separated, yet it seemed that a certain masculine atmosphere saturated the scene. It was social and enjoyable, but not intimate.What a contrast to the slow motion, gentleness, and intimacy of the Japanese *onsen*. (Of course, rituals associated with the body reflect a variety of cultural traits; for example, the Japanese obsession with cleanliness is undoubtedly reflected in the protracted soaping and washing. German vigor and thoroughness are reflected in the more athletic atmosphere of the German *bad*.)

In the West we have taken the body very seriously, but we have been afraid of it and obsessed with controlling it. In the East, historically, the body has not been taken so seriously, perhaps because there is no belief in its continuance. In fact, it has often been ignored. Both East and West have their respective dualisms that divide and afflict the body and the mind. I think in that brief time in the Japanese *onsen*, watching the women do what they have probably done for centuries, I had a glimpse of the way to the balance, to unity and harmony, to *Wa*.

On the last night in my retreat I felt poetry welling up, almost as if a door to my soul had opened up. I wrote a few lines that now seem like awkward imitations of the haiku. I realized that this creative surge came out of a synchrony of mind, body, and spirit, out of a truly *embodied knowledge*. As I fell asleep that last night I remembered the beguines, those women who chose to live in difference, their brief moment in history like a cluster of shooting stars that lit up the heavens. In the writings of the beguines there is a physicality of devotion and an affective resonance of knowledge that reflects a supremely integrated consciousness, full of soul. As Nicholson describes this gift from the past, it seems now like a challenge to us for the future:

> [The] Beguine writers envisioned love as what contemporary theorists are calling *jouissance*, a kind of boundaryless sexuality in which desire and satisfaction cannot be distinguished, just as masculine and feminine cannot be distinguished.[19]

Héléne Cixous, the feminist philosopher, has put this aspiration in contemporary terms and underscored its connection with *difference*:

> I look for a kind of desire that wouldn't be in collusion with the old story of death . . . [where] there would have to be a recognition of

each other . . . thanks to the intense and passionate work of knowing
. . . [where] each would take the risk of *other*, of *difference*, without
feeling threatened by the existence of an otherness, rather, delight-
ing to increase through the unknown what is there to discover, to
respect, to favor, to cherish.[20]

Perhaps, in the emergence of the phenomenon of the *third sex*,
these gender- nonconformists that disturb the contemporary landscape, we see the beginning of the dissolution of all dualisms and the
possibility of an evolutionary love for all men and women.

Winter skies
Mountain chill
Butterflies
Surprise.

Red leaves
On the path.
Drops of blood
Dying trees.

Morningsong.
Birds, ladies bow.
Over my tatami raft
Dreams fly.

Encounters with "the Other": The "Yang" of Teilhard de Chardin and Thomas Merton

Before 1970 the world was not much interested in the spiritual experience of women, unless they were medieval mystics or nuns. The world was even less interested in the spiritual experience of "others": in 1950 we were still measuring everything according to the experience of white men and dividing the soul from the body. These twin dualisms and the distorted perspectives they spawned left most women and those who were not privileged white males no choice but to be passive consumers of the prevailing spiritual and intellectual traditions.

Thus, in looking back to that time, I am not surprised that two of the most popular spiritual teachers of the 1950s and 1960s were men. I was just coming of age, and I was hungry for models and mentors. It never occurred to me that the experience of two white men, both of whom lived as monks, might be too narrow a frame for my own self-reflection. Indeed, the whole Western world—where the spiritual is so readily divided from the material—was perfectly willing to sit at the feet of Teilhard de Chardin and Thomas Merton and, for a time, listen attentively.

Eventually I lost interest in Teilhard and Merton when other voices—the voices of women and people of color, of the oppressed, alien voices—became more insistent in my consciousness. From the vantage point of the 1990s, however, I can see that in each of these spiritual seekers, pathfinders, there was something that echoed my own experience and forged a link with the present. Each had, in his own way, struggled with the dualism of our historical inheritance, and each had encountered *difference* in the loss and recovery of the feminine and the East.

Teilhard de Chardin's book *The Phenomenon of Man* had an overwhelming influence on my thinking around 1959 or 1960. It was probably one of the most widely read books of our time. I read it in a marathon of nights, using a flashlight so as not to disturb my dormitory mates. I had to pause often to let the words seep into my consciousness. I remember the feeling of intellectual and emotional exhilaration as I turned the pages, astonished at the complete obliteration of the tragic and troublesome flaw in the traditional Christian heritage: the Manichaean, dualistic split between matter and spirit. I found other notes I had made on the works of Teilhard de Chardin. I remembered feeling like my whole being had been opened up and the warm sap of life suddenly poured through—never again to be divided from my mind or my body.

My reaction, I am sure, was just what the Vatican's Holy Office feared when they issued a *monitum* in 1962 warning against the danger of reading Teilhard's work. It would open a Pandora's box. And it surely did in my case, and for many others as well. It was the gateway to a leap of faith in humanity and in the essential goodness of the stuff of the universe. The Fall was suddenly a leap forward, and even Evil could be transformed. Thirty-some years later the lasting impact on my own perspective and spirituality is dramatically clear.

Teilhard's work spanned the vast chasms that separated science and religion in the twentieth century and sent shock waves through the comfortable fraternities of physicists as well as theologians. He was a catalyst on many levels: a man born to Catholicism in an era of Jansenistic piety, the rage against modernism, and the fear of the body. Yet out of Teilhard's unconscious leapt a defiant affirmation that the seed of spirit is embedded in matter, and the seed of adoration and worship is embedded in science. He set in motion currents that were to lead eventually to the Second Vatican Council and to the "conversion" of science from positivism. He became a model for a new asceticism of building the earth and becoming an "artisan of progress."

The young Teilhard de Chardin was imprinted with neo-Thomism and the strict dichotomies of Aristotelian body-soul and spirit-matter distinctions. Fortunately his native infatuation with nature was encouraged by some of his teachers, and Teilhard's thinking diverged into a fascination with process and teleology. As a paleontologist and theologian, he dared to speculate about evolution and even about the validity of a concept of original sin.

Eventually his speculations led to exile, an exile that grew more absolute and cruel as the years went on. Several times in his life he was faced with the dilemma of sacrificing his ideas in order to please the hierarchy and of accepting his persona-non-grata status. He seems to have made a clear choice of the latter and never considered leaving the church, much less the Jesuits. He wrote of his sentiments and his agony to a friend, more than once: "Which is the more sacred of my vocations—the one I followed as a boy of eighteen? Or my real vocation, which I discovered when I was a man? . . . How can I obey this order without making myself the victim of the very formalism I've always stood against?"[1]

Teilhard sacrificed his right to teach and speak publicly and accepted exile from his beloved France. China was to be his destiny as well as his prison, the incubator for his most important ideas. Ironically, he was unable to transfer the integrated vision that so permeated his thinking in terms of nature and God, matter and spirit, to his perceptions of culture and gender.

Teilhard found many friends in Tientsin and Peking. Most were Europeans like himself, and even when they were Chinese, they were intellectually Westernized. His encounter was no romance with the East and he did not imagine himself as a bridge builder or missionary of any kind. He arrived in China when the country still had a feudal quality, a chaotic time when warlords still ruled the countryside and the people struck him as "primitive as 'redskins' or Australian aborigines," who lived "in a spirit of complete utilitarianism, without any kind of idealism or hope."[2] He was puzzled by the "cynical serenity" of the people and by the cycle of consolida-

tion and collapse that characterized the history of the nation. The
future of modern China was being born all around him, but he did
not seem curious enough about the mystery of this enigmatic culture to probe further. In Teilhard's mind, China would require
some "Westernization" in order to reach its full potential.

As Teilhard grew older, many of his impressions of the East
acquired a greater analogical significance. He seems to have associated the way of Life—of evolution and activity—with the West; and
the way of Entropy—death and passivity—with the East. Occasionally he admitted that elements of each could be found across cultures. Nevertheless, he held an unequivocal belief that the world
was now on the brink of making a choice for life and the dynamism
of nature, and that Christianity would be the central "phylum" of
this transformation. This led him to conclude that it was from the
West that the future would come.

Teilhard was curious about the religious heritage of the East and
visited several monasteries in search of their indigenous wisdom.
He was not persuaded of its richness and abandoned the enter-
prise, but he recognized that the East had once glimpsed something of the truth. In spite of his skepticism, he had to admit that he
was changed in subtle ways by the East, and it certainly had been a
rewarding retreat in which to nurture his ideas. He wrote to a
friend, "There is something, now, in myself, which makes me
unable to become a mere 'occidental' again."[3]

Although he worked in China for over twenty years Teilhard
never learned the language and never really integrated with the culture. Eventually he travelled to India as well as Japan. In 1947 he put
some comparative reflections in an essay called "The Spiritual Contribution of the Far East." His thoughts can never be regarded as
more than impressions, and yet these reflections come the closest
to a recognition that the East may hold wisdom which the West has
lost or never acquired. He notes that many people in the contemporary world are trying to recover a "soul," a sense of the spiritual—
and are looking Eastward to find it.

Teilhard then draws important distinctions between the spiritual traditions of India, China, and Japan. He says, "Spiritually

speaking, what makes India is an extraordinary, a predominant, sense of the one and of the divine."[4] For the Hindu the invisible is more real than the visible. He notes that the whole object of this transcendental theism is to reduce the plurality and ambiguity of life to the awareness of the One, the universal essence that underlies everything. Ultimately, Teilhard finds this way lacking because it cannot inspire true worship and love, or a genuine humanism. He believed that the weakness in Hindu spiritual philosophy was its failure to value earthly and human constructions.

In contrast to India, Teilhard found the spirit of China to be focused on the tangible, on material and human aspirations. The mysteries of the universe are regarded as impenetrable and the compelling imperative of the future is inherently suppressed. (One wonders if Teilhard's view would be the same in today's post-Mao China.) Teilhard saw China as a pragmatic, present-oriented culture. With the same procrustean sharpness, Teilhard identifies the importance of the collective consciousness in Japan—a mentality that gave rise to a mysticism of exclusivity and a spirit of sacrifice.

With more than a little cultural chauvinism but some philosophical insight, Teilhard contrasts his version of Western spirituality with the varieties in the East: instead of suppressing plurality and phenomena in order to be one with the All—as he saw the East—in the West one must "resolutely embrace the multiple, and urge it with all your energies in the direction in which it tends." Instead of seeking the God of "non-tension," one must pursue the God of tension, the dynamism of "the prime psychic mover ahead."[5] He reiterates his conviction that the West is the starting point for a spiritual "breakthrough" in our times. Nevertheless he recognizes the signs of awakening in China, where passive peasants have been converted into "death-defying proselytes," and Japan, where the best thinkers "are widening their native clan-centered ambitions to a global scale."[6]

Teilhard alluded to the "road of the East" and the "road of the West" throughout his works, but his feet were firmly planted on the Western path. He recognized that the great appeal of the Eastern traditions was their universalism and cosmic perspective. But he believed that the Buddhist and Hindu denial of matter and rejection of all pursuit of knowledge, all personalization and all earthly progress as "so many diseases of the soul" were illusion rather than wisdom. He insisted on the sublime potentiality of matter and on the evolutionary destiny of Christianity to consummate the spiritual convergence of all human consciousness.[7]

The overvaluation that limits his vision is certainly not unique to Teilhard de Chardin. It is the psychic mechanism of repression and prejudice: it forces what is *different* into the lower consciousness where it is inevitably identified as "other," as "enigma," even as "threat," and potentially "enemy." It is also the dynamic of the suppressed anima. Teilhard's notion of the universe in time is linear and teleological: it must terminate in an Omega Point. In a sense it is the triumph of monotheism. The Christification of the process of evolution is ultimately a vision that is non-inclusive and subtly contaminated with the logic of dualism.

If Teilhard's intellectual view of the East remained culture bound, on the deeply personal level he struggled to integrate his faith in matter with the contradictions of his own flesh. Pioneers and prophets can often see the "new consciousness" long before they can actualize it in their own behavior. Such contradictions are most apparent in Teilhard's view of the "feminine" and his views of sexuality.

The contradictions can only be understood by considering the context in which Teilhard experienced the "feminine" and sexuality. Born in 1881, he was the product of a very religious French family, attended a French boarding school for boys, and eventually entered the Jesuit novitiate when he was eighteen years old. Two years later, along with most other religious orders, the Jesuits were expelled from France, and Teilhard was exiled to the island of Jersey. Teilhard was assigned to do his teaching internship at the Jesuit College in Cairo.

For a young French Jesuit, Cairo must have been a sensory bazaar. But within three years Teilhard returned to England and Hastings for theological training. He was never to waiver in his commitment to the order, in spite of the persecution he endured.

The enforcement of the antimodernist agenda was nothing less than the intellectual and psychological equivalent of another Inquisition. What made Teilhard so faithful? What kept him so attached to an organization that required obedience and prohibitions that not only prevented him from teaching and sharing his intellectual ideas but also exiled him from his family and native land? Was this brilliant scientist and mystic seer also a masochist?

The answer lies, I believe, in what the Jesuits represented in his era. They were in many ways the supreme expression of the masculine religious spirit: a way of life based on superior intellectual capability, militaristic discipline, the exclusion of the feminine, a worldwide fraternity devoted to the Christification of everything. Teilhard, whose world had been saturated with male influences since he was very young, would have gained in belonging to the Jesuits an identity and status that were distinctly masculine and, therefore, implicitly superior. The Jesuits were the "Green Berets," the elite of the church, and the church and its Christology were more "advanced" than other religious traditions. As an ordinary priest or ordinary man, Teilhard could not so easily have divided the intellectual and affective dimensions, soul and body, the flesh and the spirit. Ironically, he chose a way of life that, in its rules and practices, was the antithesis of the evolutionary spirituality he imagined.

The status and superiority associated with the choice he made is evident in his relations with women. Teilhard craved their company, as his letters and habits testify. In China as well as his final years in the United States, he ritually took afternoon tea with one or more of his women friends. He often traveled with them, and most of all, allowed them to take care of many of the mundane concerns of his life. Like many other clerics and gurus, he attracted a devoted group of women who affirmed him, stimulated him, and—occasionally—inspired him. Perhaps it was the rejection by the (official) church he loved so much that made him thirsty for acceptance. American Jesuits and, no doubt, some of his more rigid French comrades were often put off by his ubiquitous retinue of women admirers—perhaps it was the obviousness of his dependency.

In his memoir of 1950, *The Heart of the Matter,* he admitted, "From the critical moment when I rejected many of the old moulds in which my family life and my religion had formed me and began to wake up and express myself in terms that were really my own, I have experienced no form of self-development without some feminine eye turned on me, some feminine influence at work."[8] He went on to describe this emotional influence as a catalyst of spiritual maturity.

In his essay and reflections entitled "Le Feminin," he seems to associate progress in love with attachment to women. After his cousin Marguerite, who first ignited his need for the feminine, it was Lucile Swan–whom he met in China–who provided the most fulfilling and problematic friendship of his life. It was Lucile who "midwifed" his books every afternoon with tea, and listened to him, questioned and critiqued, and encouraged him. She brought him a "tide of life," which he seems to have valued primarily as an energizing force for his "important" work. On many occasions, as their intimacy grew, Lucile challenged his idealistic view of celibacy. As they grew in spiritual companionship, she sensed that something more needed to be expressed: "I love you so that it hurts, which is probably not the way you want me to love you." Their intimate conversations began to end in arguments. She conceded finally: "I can't have you. Not really. So I must learn your way of having each other." But in her heart, as she told him once, she felt that his way of loving was opposed to a fundamental law of the universe.[9]

Like many men before and after who were convinced that they were born to a higher purpose, Teilhard was more comfortable with the abstract "Eternal Feminine" than with Eros in the flesh. He was forever transforming the real woman into "Beatrice." Like Dante, like Goethe, like John Paul II, the more remote the real feminine, the more the masculine consciousness projects the idealized abstract feminine. Teilhard struggled with the consequences of his emotional dualism: he missed Lucile terribly when they were separated. He waffled between his sense of guilt for "using" her and his sense of higher purpose and a more perfect love. He loved her, he said, but it had to be on his terms. There is more than a hint of superiority in his letters.

Teilhard's thoughts on "the feminine" were often rhapsodic and lyrical in the abstract. But a more realistic perception of his attitude might be gleaned from more spontaneous reactions. For example, although he was very supportive of women's equality in general, he was opposed to "disastrous egalitarianism" and "a certain form of feminism" that he called "masculinism."[10]

Teilhard's youthful reflections on virginity in his World War I wartime journal are not much different from his reflections toward the end of his life. The two key essays, "The Eternal Feminine" and "The Evolution of Chastity," reiterate the same themes: that human love is always in danger of becoming an *egoisme à deux,* and that a better, more spiritual love will transcend and transform ordinary human love, and inevitably an evolutionary variant of virginity will replace the marital state. "Marriage is always polarized socially toward reproduction, and religious perfection is always represented, theologically, in terms of separation; and there can be no doubt but that we lack a *third road* between the two. I do not mean a middle road, but a higher, a road that is demanded by the revolutionary transformation that has recently been effected in our thought by the transposition of the notion of 'spirit.'"[11]

For Teilhard, the spiritualization of matter is paralleled by the virginization of the universe. He does not see clearly how that spiritualization might take place through and with the flesh—probably because that was not his experience. Teilhard remained a dualist in respect to human love precisely because he remained a Jesuit: he was convinced that celibacy was a higher, more perfect way. Beneath the sense of superiority is the reality of the fear of the feminine, a fear of engulfment, a fear of loss of control.

When Teilhard circulated his essay on chastity to his circle of friends, the response was not enthusiastic. His old friend and fellow Jesuit Valensin wrote to him—with undisguised exasperation—that in regard to this particular aspect of human experience, Teilhard hadn't the faintest idea what he was talking about.[12]

Another dualism that Teilhard sought to collapse, but where

again he only partially succeeded, was the paradox of life and death. This most fundamental dichotomy was the underlying theme of his early book *The Divine Milieu*. Teilhard's evolutionary spirituality organized all the pain, suffering, and struggle of human endeavor in a constellation of "little deaths," which he called the "passivities of diminishment." Friendly and favorable forces he identified as "passivities of growth." Attachment and detachment were inextricably intertwined in the spiritual life, which mimicked the life of nature. He imagined a universe in which not only were spirit and matter one and the same stuff ultimately, but in which the forces of life and death were equally valued and necessary in the inexorable fulfillment of the destiny of the soul as well as creation.

When Teilhard reaches the ultimate point of convergence, the question of the life, death, and/or transformation of the universe, his thought seems to stumble. As a scientist, he could accept that entropy was one of the laws of the universe, a cosmic "passivity of diminishment." Physicists have predicted that the inexorable process of increasing entropy must finally lead to the "death of heat," and then a cold, lifeless universe—perhaps absolute reduction to maximum density, a black hole. Teilhard's law of increasing "complexification" and consciousness runs counter to entropy, a contradictory evolutionary force.

In order to justify his theory, Teilhard must deny the possibility of cosmic death. A total death of the life system as we know it is radically incompatible with the goal of evolution; therefore, Teilhard insists there must be "a point of escape from space and time."[13] This is precisely the teleology of the Omega Point, which he has described in *The Phenomenon of Man*, *The Future of Man*, and other works.

What would Teilhard think today? The question pricks our imaginative curiosity. We at least have some very noteworthy speculation that challenges his theory. Frank Tipler, a physicist, has proposed a countertheory in his book *The Physics of Immortality*, which suggests that the total death of the universe may actually be a condition of its resurrection. Tipler's theory is highly speculative. In his view, the Earth's culture and civilization, and all the individuals who have ever existed, will necessarily be converted from a finite reality to a virtual reality, from real space to the cyberspace of a computer's memory before the collapse of the universe—only to be resurrected by the intentionality of the doomed life system. An astonishing theory, to say the least. But it seems very much like a theory sprung from the disembodied brain of a Zeus-like Western science.

Perhaps the most eloquent and persuasive answer comes from the subjugated knowledge of the Earth itself. New voices are being heard, voices that remind us that all beings are one and of equal value; that all things are connected, and that we will find survival and flourishing of life in relationship; and finally, that life and death are but different phases of an unseen harmony that we are struggling toward.

It is easy from the vantage point of the 1990s to find flaws in the grand synthesis that was the focus of Teilhard de Chardin's unique existence. What is significant is that his blind spots are precisely the places where crucial breakthroughs are occurring today and will occur in the near future. Particularly in his love-hate perspectives in relation to the East and to the Feminine we may find the roots of our own convergence. He could see that something new, something as feminine as the earth itself, was bursting through the crust of civilization and surging up out of the depths of his own being.

In 1928 when Teilhard de Chardin was leaving France for China Thomas Merton was leaving France for England. Eventually Merton would also find a "road to the East," but in a very different way. Although born thirty-four years apart, both of these great seekers seemed to have absorbed some of the spiritual intensity of the land of their birth. Their lives overlap in a fortuitous way: Teilhard perhaps the first contemporary challenge to a moribund spirituality, Merton a long-distance runner who picked up the baton of the fallen warrior and plunged into his own unique version of a spiritual renaissance.

In contrast to Teilhard, I never counted Merton as one of my spiritual fathers. The most I could say is that his autobiography and writing up to 1968 influenced me and intrigued me, but my interest in him did not survive his death. By 1970 the women's movement and the profound developments in epistemology, as well as theology and spirituality, swept over many of us and carried us in new directions. Yet looking back now, I can see that Thomas Merton was a kind of spiritual director for a whole generation— my generation. He was an epiphenomenon as well as paradigm for the great influx of young people into religious communities in the decade of the 1950s, part of a post–World War II religious revival. He was our Augustine, and in many ways his own conflicts mirrored and prophesied ours. We had lived through and mythologized the "good war." He was one of the first lonely voices to announce that there were no "good wars," and he was silenced for a time for saying so, and saying so often.

But now, looking back at his meaning from the distance of twenty-five years, I have a renewed interest in several aspects of his life: the role of the feminine, his interest in the spirituality of the East, and the meaning of his death.

I see Merton's spiritual journey in three stages. The first stage, beginning with his conversion, was a very Augustinian period marked by detachment, dualism, and a rock-hard ball of self-doubt and self-hatred lodged deep in his soul. The second phase was an existential period, the intellectual struggle to understand the human condition and to shape the self, the project of "becoming" what he was not. And finally, only near the very end of his life, a sapiential phase, the recovery of "being" and the original unity. Toward the end his spirituality shifted in its orientation from Logos to Eros, and he seemed to be moving toward a reintegration of the feminine.

One overall impression of Merton's life that seems inescapable is the absence of the feminine, especially of close, sustained contact with real women. There is no question that Merton was under-mothered, that is, lacking an intense, intimate bond with a powerful female presence, sustained over a period of time. The brief portrait of his mother that appears in his autobiography is sketched in tones of deprivation. He remembers her being disappointed in him, critical and distant. During her long illness with cancer, she never allowed him to visit her in the hospital. She died when Merton was six, leaving a diary which—when Merton read it later—confirmed many of his impressions of the lack in their relationship. Yet we see in his mother's intense introspection and unrelenting habit of diary-writing something that impacted on her son. In trying to make sense of her own experience, this enigmatic woman shaped her son's inclination to self-analysis.

Merton had few playmates and no sisters. His only sibling, a brother, was killed in the war. After the death of his mother, his life was a succession of changing locations and boys' schools as his father wandered about two continents. Looking at his situation from a contemporary psychological viewpoint, one might conclude that his early "holding environment" and protofemininity were compromised. "Protofemininity" is a word used in some psychological circles to describe an intense connection and experience with the feminine which begins in the womb, continues through infancy and early childhood, and is considered to be the core of the psyche.[14]

In terms of object relations he was thrown very early into an increasingly and exclusively male world. This is perhaps why most of Merton's lifelong friends and correspondents were men, and why women were not very significant as peers in his experience. When women do appear in his memoirs or other writings, they are either exotic creatures, attractive and seductive, or they are simply not very important. They are almost always women cast in certain "roles." In fact, he often refers to women as "girls," and usually leaves them unnamed in his writing— remarkable for one who was an inveterate name-dropper. (To what extent monastic censorship may have encouraged this is a question.)

In understanding a person's spirituality it is important to understand the psychology that is its ground. At the core of Merton's spirituality was an undeniable fear and dread of the feminine, and at the same time a vulnerability to its seduction. The choice of the monastic life would be a natural defensive maneuver for someone with this disposition. Essentially a flight from female power, it is also a flight from the sensual, the natural, the emotional, the concrete, the immanent, and the real.

While we may never know all the particulars, we see a pattern of flight in Merton's life beginning with his departure from Cambridge under mysterious circumstances. Merton himself alludes to this event with overtones of guilt throughout his life. Apparently there was a scandal when a young woman was pregnant by him. Merton escaped to America, with the encouragement of his guardian. On his last journey to Asia he confided to a friend that he had an affair with a girl who made the beds in his Cambridge dormitory and she had a baby. Merton was unsure if they had survived the war, but remarked that his son would be thirty-something now. Clearly it was a load he carried to the end of his life, and, according to his Asian companion, it was somehow the key to his story.[15]

Catholicism and then monasticism offered Merton a way to redeem himself and at the same time an escape into abstraction and asceticism. Jung was not the only philosopher or psychologist who has observed that the more distanced a man is from the real and concrete feminine, the more intense is his yearning for an "eternal feminine," a projection of a maternal character onto certain social institutions that are perceived as nurturing and empowering. Thus the church, the religious order, the alma mater of the university, personifications of science, ideology, and nations function as maternal archetypes in the consciousness of men distanced from women and, often as not, from their own feelings. In eras, cultures, and psyches where the power of the real feminine has been eclipsed, we should not be surprised to see the flight to the monastery or Mariology.

Feminist philosophers who have examined this displacement suggest that fear and alienation from the feminine are so deeply rooted in the normative Anglo male that he is alienated from himself, and the recovery of his authentic self must intrinsically involve the recovery of a relation to the real feminine. Merton's life certainly gives credence to the hypothesis that "to an extent, the so-called unconscious is historically censored femaleness."[16]

One of Merton's lesser-known works, a prose poem called

"Hagia Sophia," takes on added significance in the light of this perspective. An artist-friend of Merton had a painting that depicted a woman (presumably Mary) crowning the young Christ. Merton's friend was not sure how to interpret the painting and inquired what Thomas Merton thought about it. In a letter to the artist in 1959 Merton said the figure was Holy Wisdom (Sophia), the feminine aspect of God. And thus the Virgin Mary, who conferred humanity upon the Word of God, is the created person who most manifests the hidden Wisdom of God.[17] This insight, as well as Merton's recurring dreams about a woman whom he identified as Wisdom, seems to have been the catalyst for the "Hagia Sophia," published a couple of years later. The poem is an extended meditation on the feminine aspect of God through the complex symbolism of Wisdom/Eve/Mary/Anima/God as Mother. Throughout the poem Merton addresses Wisdom as his Sister.

The poem opens with a very lyrical passage describing the presence of Wisdom at the dawn of creation. Merton then injects himself into the scene:

> This is at once my own being, my own nature, and the Gift of my
> Creator's Thought and Art within me, speaking as Hagia Sophia,
> speaking as my sister,
> Wisdom.
> I am awakened, I am born again at the voice of this my Sister, sent to
> me from the depths of the divine fecundity.

Then Merton pictures himself lying asleep in a hospital; he is dreaming in the early hours of the morning when the gentle voice of a nurse awakens him. Merton compares the experience to Adam being awakened by Eve. He is "beginning to be made whole":

> Love takes him by the hand, and opens to him the doors of another
> life, another day.[18]

Further on in the poem Merton reflects on Sophia, Wisdom, as a manifestation of God as Mother. "Perhaps," Merton says, "she is even the Divine Nature, the One in Father, Son, and Holy Ghost." He sees Sophia as the manifestation of God in the world, the feminine principle that makes God's grace present in creation. The

archetypal imagery and power of this poem signal the eclipse of
Merton's Augustinian phase and a new spiritual hunger arising in
the depths of his soul. Meanwhile he immersed himself in an existential quest.

As the years passed in the monastery, Merton's desire for solitude was disturbed by his social conscience. Even on the last day of
his life, in Bangkok, he was still conscious of his own struggle to balance "world refusal" and "world acceptance" in his life. As his dialog with the world accelerated, the focus of his concern shifted
from self-loathing to social criticism. He publicly challenged many
of the values and events of his time. War, poverty, racism evoked his
passionate involvement. Gandhi, Tolstoy, Thoreau, Camus shaped
his emerging existential solidarity. Coinciding with this existential
immersion in the issues of his time, Merton experienced another
kind of conversion, his famous Fourth-and-Walnut epiphany in
1958—a breakthrough realization of the essential oneness of
humanity and the illusion of difference. In the middle of a shop-
ping center at Fourth and Walnut in Louisville, Merton is overwhelmed by a sense of oneness with all of humanity. He awakens
from "a dream of separateness" and from the illusion of a separate
holy existence.[19]

From this time on Merton was no longer preoccupied with
"what he was not," but had now discovered that the key to his own
"becoming" was to be found in "connecting." This growing existential openness required his own liberation from oppressive structures, and he was finally allowed to live as a hermit, or in other
words, to live apart from the community and yet still be of it. He
could never again hide behind the persona provided by normative
Trappist life.

Within a year of his move to the hermitage in 1965 he was hospi-
talized and met his Sophia/Eve in the flesh, a young nurse who
seems to have been a perfect receptor for Merton's unconscious
projections. Merton was obviously in a transitional state of mind.
He fell deeply in love with this woman, who, significantly, was only
identified as "S." in the biographic material. Merton seems to have
been so in love with her that he risked a great deal of exposure in

order to continue the relationship after he returned to Gethsemani. It was soon found out, and, once again, Merton sought an escape route, made easier because she was not—apparently—pregnant and was thirty years his junior.

This intense relationship was undoubtedly a pivotal event for Thomas Merton. The cracks were beginning to appear in his abstract inner mythology; in his flight from immanence he suddenly found himself bogged down in earthliness. He was growing more critical of the church, which he once compared to Kafka's Castle. He was beginning to "see through" the institutionalized monastic life. His attachment to the Ideal was in the process of transformation into recognition of the Real; his longing for the idealized feminine converged upon the concrete woman—the lost sister, companion, and lover. The anima buried in Merton was making itself known.

During this period he had an exchange of letters with Rosemary Ruether that are remarkable for the level of self-disclosure that she evoked from Merton. They discuss the church as having hardened into an idol. She accuses Merton of being an escapist; he accuses her of being too "cerebral." She questions his asceticism as life-denying. He is completely honest with her that his goal is a spiritual liberty and that he has had a great struggle with his religious commitment.[20]

These letters are exceptional, one of the few times that one sees Merton sparring with a woman as his equal, gloves off, roles cast aside. Ruether was one on whom he would have difficulty projecting a more comfortable idealized or romantic feminine. He sheds, at least for a time, both his anima and his animus complex.

During this same two-year period he wrote to a male friend about the difficulties of sublimation. He admits he has been in love since entering the monastery. He is not sure if chastity and sublimation are not a huge mistake, but he honestly thinks it is his fate. There are hints in the writing and correspondence of this period that he discovered that love cannot be sought, that it is a gift, given unconditionally. Merton's letters to the young woman he loved have never surfaced (to my knowledge), and it is generally believed that he destroyed them before his trip to Asia. We can guess at the state of his feelings from some of the arcane and not so arcane allusions in the poetry of this period. But it seems as if this love had finally dissolved much of the ball of self-hatred that lodged in Merton's heart. Sophia now had a human face.

The affair with the nurse and the kind of exchange he had with Ruether indicate a new level of awareness. It is no longer fear of women and guilt for having abandoned some, but now a real questioning of what he called his "refusal of women." The unconscious longing to make contact with and free the buried feminine in himself was now conscious and connected with the acceptance of real women. He sensed, I think, that here there was an opening to the divine. He begins to shed his persona and to strip away all the false transcendence and abstraction. He is ready for a descent into immanence when he leaves on his last journey. He goes in search of his "original unity" and the integration of the parts of himself that have been warring for years. All his life Merton had pursued his anima in fleeting specters that vanished. (He, of course, was the conjuror that made them vanish!). Now the impact of this crisis makes him take flight again, this time to Asia. But it is also a flight toward something.

Merton's interest in the East began during his years at Columbia University, probably as a result of reading Aldous Huxley. Huxley's *Ends and Means* stimulated an interest in Eastern mysticism. Merton began to read many Oriental texts. But the seeds fell on "stony ground" in the late 1930s and early 1940s. Neither Merton nor the world was quite ready for enlightenment from the East. Nevertheless, Merton's encounter during these years with the Hindu monk Bramachari and their subsequent friendship were to have a lasting effect. His repeated advice to Merton and his friends, "Seek your own roots," nudged Merton in the direction of Western mysticism. When Merton began to read the fathers of the church, something took root in him, and the foundations of his spiritual journey were laid.

Within a few years Merton entered the Trappists and continued his journey as a monk. During these years, as one biographer points out, Merton

> steeped himself in the church fathers, the fathers of the desert, the Cistercian writers of the twelfth century, and the great fourteenth- and sixteenth-century mystics. It was his reading of these classics of Christian spirituality that eventually—though not immediately—turned his mind and heart once again in the direction of the East . . . he had to find the East in the West before he could discover the East in himself.[21]

By the 1960s Merton was engaged in dialogs with John Wu, D. T. Suzuki, Thich Nhat Hanh, and other artisans and archaeologists of Eastern spirituality. In his *Zen and the Birds of Appetite* Merton noted that the impact of Zen on the West struck with full force after World War II, almost as a response to the existential alienation of the times, the beginning of the atomic and cybernetic age, when Western religion and philosophy were in a state of crisis.

Of all the Eastern traditions, Merton gravitated most of all toward Zen. He found in Zen a "way" rather than a doctrine, a consciousness and awareness rather than a kerygma and redemption. In Zen and its links with Taoism, and to some extent Buddhism, Merton found a principle of unity, an escape from Western dualism and the one-dimensional mind of the West. In *Zen and the Birds of Appetite* he describes it as, "a breakthrough, an explosive liberation from a one-dimensional conformism, a recovery of unity which is not the suppression of opposites, but a simplicity beyond opposites . . . a primal simplicity."[22]

In these years that verged on the precipice of his premature death, two aspects of his imprisoned anima—the feminine and the wisdom of the East—seem to have converged in a spiritual epiphany within his own consciousness. His final journey to Asia provided a remarkable confirmation of this convergence and his liberation.

In *Zen and the Birds of Appetite* Merton had discussed, in the abstract, the possibility of an integrating transcendent experience in his characteristic analytical style. The discovery of the "original unity, the face which you had before you were born" is an experience in which one does not see Buddha, but that one is Buddha, and Buddha is not what the images in the temple or tradition lead one to expect. In his *Asian Journal* Merton records a personal encounter with the great stone images of Buddha at Polonnaruwa in Sri Lanka in more personal terms. No abstraction here; only the immediacy of transcendence and wholeness. It is a moment of transcendence and epiphany. He knows he will never be the same again: "[Here] my Asian pilgrimage has come clear and purified itself. I mean, I know and have seen what I was obscurely looking for. I don't know what else remains but I have now seen and have pierced through the surface and have got beyond the shadow and the disguise."[23]

Merton extended his mystical experience by living for a few days in the Tibetan jungle-forest as a recluse. Later in Calcutta he participated with great exuberance in the Hindu festival and rituals of Kali, the great goddess of life and death. This meeting of Merton with the Dark Goddess seems especially symbolic of the spiritual passage he had entered.

In the worship of the Goddess Kali, the seeker must confront the meaning of death in its most concrete form. Kali is both the loving mother, the creatrix who gives birth and nourishes, and the destroyer, the devourer of flesh who dances on corpses. She is always pictured in ways that terrify the onlooker, dripping with blood, with a necklace of skulls, and the like. Gruesome as she may appear, she is worshiped as the source of power and strength, of equality and justice. Her fierce laughter and blissful smile—the paradox of her symbolism—make no sense to Western logic and the Cartesian mind. She makes complete sense to the enlightened mind, to one who has recaptured the original unity. Merton's fascination with her mirrors his final spiritual, sapiential passage and the meaning of his death.

Shortly before his untimely death from accidental electrocution in Bangkok in 1968, Merton announced a decision to remain in Asia for a while in order to learn the Tibetan Buddhist discipline of Dzogchen. On several occasions previously he had expressed admiration for the most famous "scripture" of Tibetan Buddhism, *The Tibetan Book of the Dead,* which is better known in Tibet as *The Great Book of Natural Liberation through Understanding in the Between.* Jung has called it "an initiation process whose purpose is to restore to the soul the divinity, the unity it lost at birth."[24]

Merton learned many things in the short time he was exposed to the practitioners of Tibetan Buddhism and Dzogchen. In those last weeks he seemed to be disassembling the dualistic infrastructure of his mind and heart, resurrecting his anima. Dzogchen is a method of self-liberation and teaches a process through death, and a recognition of the continuity of life and death. This remarkable convergence in Merton of masculine and feminine, of West and East, reached a crescendo in the synthesis of life and death that seems to have been the final revelation of his life. The meeting with the goddess Kali and with Dzogchen were signs of a transformation that would prepare him for the final passage and rebirth.

The unity of life and death is a truth that the Western world has long forgotten. Joseph Campbell, in his landmark study of mythology, described what he called the Great Reversal, a shift in cultural values around the second millennium B.C.E. that divided life and death in the consciousness of humanity.[25] Death was no longer viewed as the continuation of the wonder of life, as a passage to another birth, but as the termination of life, the release from a world of pain and suffering. By the third millennium, war and an emerging patriarchal order had displaced the goddesses that symbolically and ritually integrated life and death. In modern times, having grown used to the separation of life and death, we have gone even further and decided to do away with death and suffering. The goal of all medical science, in fact, seems to be the extinction of pain and death. Death and pain are synonymous with disease and disorder, malignancies that must be eliminated. The denial of death, the extinction of death—in such a world Kali's return is inevitable. There are many signs today that we are in the process of a theophany, a reappearance and resurgence of the Dark Mother, the archetypal aspect of the feminine that represents the repressed, denigrated half of ourselves and the soul of the culture. The Dark Mother, Kali, is bursting through our divided, hypnotized consciousness—as she did in Thomas Merton.

Teilhard de Chardin and Thomas Merton are hardly typical of ordinary sojourners on the spiritual path, but their widespread influence in the mid-twentieth century coincided with the apogee of the Western consciousness and the techno-scientific era. The analytical gift of the West, the binary logic and the rationalized, masculinized culture that brought us into the modern era reached a climax in Hiroshima in 1946. The achievement had been purchased at a cost: the avoided, repressed, rejected values of the feminine, the *yin* swallowed up by the *yang*. Hiroshima was the beginning of the post-modern era, and the questioning of the Great Reversal. Teilhard and Merton were not typical, but they were very representative of this apogee of the Western consciousness. By education, by choice of life-style, in their thinking frameworks, they were paradigmatic expressions of the Western spirit. Each pursued his soul on a path that was, in part, the scaling of a mountain and, in part, a flight. Teilhard de Chardin sought wholeness and integration in his mystical/scientific synthesis of the unity of matter and spirit. Merton found his in a final immersion in Eastern wisdom.

Today we can look further than their horizons for spiritual paradigms and the wisdom of a lived experience.

Skin
Hanging in melting shreds.
Thousands plunge over bridge, banks
River of fire
River of death.

No smiles
No wink.
Irony sleeps
Only badger breaks
The spell.

Mountain stream
Garden of stones
White water illusion
Purity.

Journey into Difference: The "Yin" of Mary Catherine Bateson, Audre Lorde, and Joanna Macy

Since childhood I have been a pilgrim to foreign lands and far-away places. When I was young, it was chiefly excursions through books that fascinated me. I remember devouring stories of children who lived different lives in countries I had never seen. In my imagination they became fascinating playmates, pen pals with whom I corresponded but whose letters never arrived. In my adulthood, I could live out those fantasies, as my writing and lecturing little by little took me to other cultures and other climes.

It was in Japan that I first felt the shock of being a Westerner. And it was in Japan that I came face to face with the shadow that lies over our own United States history: racism. In a country as homogeneous as Japan, it takes you by surprise. The politeness, the courtesy, and the decorum of the Japanese make the visitor feel spoiled. I came to enjoy all the bows and *-sans* and service. I felt honored and admired in many of my encounters with those who knew who I was and why I was there. But if I transgressed the psychic space between us and moved too close to personal sharing, I suddenly felt a curtain descend. This was not America, where one can have a very personal conversation with the mail carrier or with an anonymous passenger sitting next to one on a plane. Gradually I could feel something akin to what black people in the United States must feel all the time, the projection of *difference*.

To be a *gaijin*, a Westerner, an outsider, in Japan is to be intensely conscious of attitudes that range from feelings of fear, to superiority, to racism. One encounter especially stands out in my mind. I was taking the bullet train from Nagoya to Hiroshima, and a small Japanese boy was loose in the aisle, occasionally showing his toy to another passenger. He visited several other passengers before he arrived at my row and began to chatter. I made conversation in as universal a language as I could. Suddenly his mother jumped out of her seat and dragged him away. I caught the repetition of the word *gaijin* twice. I felt like a leper.

Another encounter in Hiroshima at the Peace Museum reminded me of what it could mean to be a foreigner in Japan. I was admiring a beautiful sculpture outside the museum, a sculpture of a woman fleeing the holocaust of the bomb, one child on her back and another clutched in her hand. A gentleman who spoke English told me that the sculpture was a memorial to the thousands of Koreans, slave laborers, who were killed or maimed by the bomb. My informant explained it was a recent addition to the Peace Memorial Park, because it had taken so long for the Japanese to acknowledge consciously that there were others—hostages—who also suffered the same fate as the Japanese.

Cathy Davidson, an American teacher who spent many years in Japan, has observed, "Typically, Japanese are happy to discuss American racism but blind to the equivalent prejudice in their own country."[1] American businessmen are warned about Japanese "ethnic, nationalist xenophobia."[2] Japanese prejudice is particularly cruel toward the *burakumin* (Japan's untouchable caste), the Ainu (Japanese indigenous people), Koreans (who are still denied citizenship), and Filipinos. Nor are other cultures exempt from this prejudice. Illegal immigrants, who do much of the low-paying labor in Japan, fuel the racist paranoia. For example, a national police memo warns that Pakistanis have "a unique body odor and carry infectious diseases."[3]

In one of the most costly political gaffes in Japan's post–World War II history, Prime Minister Nakasone set off reactions around the world when he remarked in a 1986 speech that "in America there are many blacks, Puerto Ricans and Mexicans, and on the average America's level [of intelligence] is still extremely low."[4]

With a naivete incomprehensible to ears chastened by political cor-
rectness, Nakasone's explanation of Japan's productive superiority
as the result of a combination of speed, information, and racially
pure intelligence sent shock waves throughout the global economy
and international governments. Presumably, heterogeneous and
racially divided cultures were to be regarded as underdeveloped.
Not since World War II had international ears heard these ideas so
explicitly announced. Nakasone's "rising sun" soon became a sun-
set on the world scene.

A recent study of Japanese racism traces its virulence to fixation
on a sense of racial superiority and Japan's need to establish the
"otherness" of everyone else on earth.[5] Some of this can no doubt
be traced to Japan's history of purging its own indigenous people.
The archipelago once belonged to the aboriginal Ainu, the *emishi.*
The warrior class, *samurai,* seems to have had its origins in this
compulsion to exterminate the *emishi.* A few historians have
recently traced much of Japan's native religion and mythology to
the rich imaginative heritage of these indigenous people, whose
poetic and animistic spirit illuminated the natural world. One
Japanese writer laments, "So deeply rooted was this discrimination
that its legacy is seen in Japanese society to this day, in an attitude of
fear and loathing toward other cultures that remind us of the
emishi."[6]

In reinventing themselves after World War II the Japanese
strongly identified with the Jews, "a chosen people" who were inno-
cent victims of a holocaust. On the other hand, anti-Semitic literature is prolific and popular in Japan. Perhaps this need to prove
superiority is also the root of the Japanese obsession with how they
are viewed by non-Japanese. The Japanese have been called "the
most pathologically self-reflective and self-conscious people in the
world."[7] As booksellers can testify, they devour Westerners' reflections on them and sustain a whole subgenre of literature devoted to
this analysis.

So it was with a great sense of irony that, in spite of being
immersed in a society that is organized to produce a sense of
belonging, loyalty, connection, and inclusion, I—as *gaijin,* a for-

eigner—knew I was doomed to isolation and, in the long run, a projected feeling of inferiority, if I remained long in that culture. This general observation, however, was offset by the many genuine experiences of connection that I had with individual Japanese who sought me out for conversation. Had I been able to speak Japanese, those conversations might have been multiplied, but it would not have changed my status as *gaijin*.

I left Japan with a great sense of having received many gifts: gifts of friendship and of spiritual insight. But I arrived home with a new appreciation for the one gift that Japan is lacking and that America possesses in abundance: tolerance for diversity and *difference*. While the melting pot is a lofty ideal and our behavior often belies our belief, nevertheless we live and move and breathe a basic openness, which few other cultures possess. Above all, as a society, we are open to possibility and novelty and interchange. Historically, *difference* has been a source of growth and development. The current paranoia about immigrants and migrant labor comes out of fear rather than out of our indigenous national character. But tolerance is a virtue that requires eternal vigilance, or it can be lost.

The encounter with the East led me to further reflection on the meaning of *difference* for the spiritual journey. When I am contemplating such matters I tend to go to nature to see what wisdom it has to offer. It is often in the behavior of the most fundamental unit of life, the cell, that we find analogs and sometimes answers to our questions about human life and history. In thinking about *difference*, I was reminded of the new knowledge about the immune system that science has discovered.

The rapid growth of the human population, the crowding together of many individuals in urban areas, the existence of high-speed, efficient means of travel and communication, the disappearance of natural predators because of "development," medical advances in drugs—all of these factors have changed our relationship to each other as well as to viruses, bacteria, and parasites. The changes present an unparalleled challenge to our immune system. In evolutionary terms, the immune system has always served the sole purpose of defense against foreign invaders, defense against *difference*. The immune system itself seems to have developed because of another inherent characteristic of life: adaptation and the capacity to convert competition between pathogen and host into a cooperative coexistence.[8] The most successful species have developed this capacity more than others. Scientists believe that viral mutations confirm this capacity and expect that even the HIV virus and its human host may eventually evolve such a cooperative coexistence. Thus, the challenge of *difference* seems to be a catalyst of growth and strength, of the persistence of life itself.

Difference also seems to be the key to the development of consciousness. Gregory Bateson states a profound philosophical, physiological, and spiritual truth when he says, "The interaction between parts of mind is triggered by *difference*."[9] In reading the works of his daughter, Mary Catherine Bateson, I am struck with her articulation of this reality, beginning with her origins as a child of two very disparate personalities, Margaret Mead and Gregory Bateson. She writes very much out of her own experience—in contrast to her father's abstract mindscape—and extracts the wisdom of a life lived in a changing scene of people, places, and cultures.

Bateson is one of several contemporary women whose spiritual experience provides an interesting contrast to the masculine paradigm of earlier times, or to the example of a Teilhard or a Thomas Merton. Recalling the encouragement to write stories and poems she received as a child, Bateson remembers a fairy tale that she dictated to her mother. It was about a sad, dreary kingdom that had no colors. The heroine of the story is a princess who has a special gift, the gift to see colors and differences where everyone else saw sameness. The princess succeeds in teaching everyone else in the kingdom how to see color and transforms their ability to understand and enjoy life.[10] The fairy tale is the story of the author, who learned from a very early age and from multiple events how to appreciate *difference*. Mary Catherine Bateson was a schoolgirl during the years she lived in Israel, a young wife when she went to the Philippines, and a new mother when she moved to Iran. These experiences, as well as her unusual childhood, gave her new eyes to interpret a life pattern: "Adaptation comes out of encounters with novelty that may seem chaotic."[11] She makes sense of the way difference and diversity are integrated with sameness and continuity in a kind of double-helix view of how organisms grow and develop as a result of new learning:

> To get outside of the imprisoning framework of assumptions learned within a single tradition, habits of attention and interpretation need to be stretched and pulled and folded back upon themselves, life lived along a Mobius strip. These are lessons too complex for a single encounter, achieved by garnering doubled and often contradictory visions rather than by replacing one set of ideas with another. When the strange becomes familiar, what was once obvious may become obscure. The goal is to build a complex structure in which both sets of ideas are intelligible, a double helix of tradition and personal growth.[12]

Life, in her view, is essentially "an improvisatory art," necessary for "a world in which we are increasingly strangers and sojourners." She defines her identity as that of "a wanderer, who is, at the deepest level, not estranged, carrying and sustaining a sense of home."[13]

In her search for a spiritual paradigm, Bateson discovers the story of Ruth from the Bible. In many ways it is her own story, having lived in many cultures, married an Armenian, and adapted to new cultural expectations many times: "It had not occurred to me how much the capacity to combine new roles to create an innovative and integrated whole might depend on exposure to another culture."[14]

Ruth's story is a paradigm for the spiritual seeker of our time. Two women, Ruth the Moabite woman and Naomi, her Hebrew mother-in-law, are refugees. They are two widows; there are no surviving children, and there are no other men in the clan to whom they can "belong." Naomi decides that her life is so bitter that she must return to her homeland, to Bethlehem. Ruth could return to her mother's house, but she pledges herself to be Naomi's companion. There is a bond between them, in spite of difference in culture, age, religion, and circumstance. Each woman takes the risk of stepping out of an expected role and out of a certain cultural perspective. When Boaz sees Ruth gleaning in the fields near Bethlehem, he is attracted to Ruth because of her devotion to Naomi. The rest is history and the Hebrew genealogy from Jesse to Jesus.

The story of Ruth challenges the paradigm of the traditional male hero who must seek his destiny or spiritual redemption in the archetypal pattern: he must go alone, depending only on his wits or his magic weapon to survive the trials. The goal is clear; the ending is always in sight. He goes to the underworld or goes to war (leaving his wife behind) or dons a disguise and goes into the forest. His end is foreshadowed in his beginning—he does not undergo radical change of context and perspective. Not so with Ruth, or with most women. They are rarely alone; others go with them. They have no weapons or magic; they follow their heart and intuition as much as their head. They remain rooted in reality and in relationship. They improvise, because they are continually encountering change and *difference*. Indeed, they often change their minds, their perspectives, their life-styles. Bateson points out how women's lives today are different:

> The traditional tales of [male] achievement or of conversion, whatever suspense and danger were built in along the way, were always cultural constructions, fabricated to make the confusing realities of life fit in with ideas like salvation or progress. . . . In my recent work on the ways women combine commitments to career and family, I have been struck by how commonly women zigzag from stage to stage without a long-term plan, improvising along the way, building the future from "something old and something new."[15]

For those who seek a spiritual path today, we perhaps have more to learn from the unacknowledged wisdom of women than from the "fathers" and "masters" of the past. The lives of most people are becoming more and more like the stories of Ruth, of women: "It is only after many surprises and choices, interruptions and disappointments, that I have arrived somewhere I could never have anticipated."[16]

The crazy quilts of women's lives and women's skill in improvising their lives may be the *subjugated knowledge* most needed for a sustainable society and a survivable future. Men's lives have been distinctly different; they have had the luxury of specializing, of single-minded focus, of abstraction, of having to play only one or two roles—provider and father/boss—which are carefully circumscribed. Women get used to interruptions and emergencies; they have to maintain multiple levels of focus. They store and process information in nonlinear ways; their attention is global. Women who are simultaneously wives, sisters, mothers, caretakers for parents, workers, household managers, providers, chauffeurs, volunteer corps for causes, and support to other women develop a "peripheral vision." Their thinking is more context-dependent, and more provisional than men's.

How this might fit women for the business of the future is becoming more evident. "Learning is the new continuity for individuals; innovation the new continuity for business."[17] A recent study of women in management in the *Harvard Business Review* found that successful women managers had very different attributes from their male peers. These women had a more interactive, cooperative, and *improvisational* style. This style requires a more flexible ego than male managers have generally exhibited. The study found that the successful women managers were different from most of their male predecessors; and, more significantly, they were not found in the Fortune 500 companies. They were in companies that were fast changing, entrepreneurial, international, and service oriented—the types of companies that are the companies of the future. An article in *Healthcare Forum Journal* states:

> The kinds of organizations that we will see in the future . . . will be rapidly changing organizations with an ad hoc flavor, aligned with one group at one time for one kind of function, working alone for another function, linking up in all kinds of different work relationships. People are going to be sharing jobs. A lot of bare-bones organizations will be contracting out a lot of work. It's an image of constant change.[18]

The future will demand more improvisational people. The economy of the future will have fewer "jobs" and more "tasks," and the tasks will be constantly shifting. Women and minorities seem to bring more of this new style as well as different content to the work-

place. Does *difference* make a difference? Kathleen Black of the
Gannett newspaper chain believes it does. The Gannett chain has
what is probably the most diverse editorial staff of any news organization. She has been known to remark that, if there weren't so
many women and people of color on the editorial staff of *USA
Today*, it would have to be called *USA Yesterday*.[19] International
field workers have also observed the variation in women's adaptive
skills in less-developed countries. Their greater sensitivity to the
environment (trees, water, animal life) as well as to human welfare
marks them as *animadores*—"animators, energizers"—of a sustainable future.

> Fluidity and discontinuity are central to the reality in which we live.
> Women have always lived discontinuous and contingent lives. . . . By
> examining the way women have coped with discontinuities in their
> lives, we may discover important clues that will help us all, men and
> women, cope with our unfolding lives.[20]

Another woman whose life encompassed multiple dimensions
of *difference*, a woman who articulated difference, lived it and symbolized it more than most others, was Audre Lorde. Poet, philosopher, black, mother, lesbian, feminist, activist—this uncommon
woman succumbed in her prime to a common fate of women in
our time: breast cancer. She was often the first voice, sometimes
the only voice, at critical moments of revelation, when consciousness and conscience were gradually awakening.

In the early years of the black power movement, she saw the sexism within the movement before whites or blacks could see it. She
gave it a name and a language to explain it. She had the power,
through her writing and speaking, to shock others into awareness.
Sometimes she acted. In the late 1960s few knew that she was a
lesbian until the day she tacked her "Love Poem" to the door of her
office. One friend remembers, "I heard the reverberations from
coast to coast."[21] It was an era when to be black and homosexual
was seen as treason to the black revolution, "to be tainted with
white evil." She made women of color realize that when black men

spoke about black liberation and when theologians spoke about liberation theology women were not included.

It was a wake-up call for all women. "Like other women, I had been mute, silenced by the black rhetoric of the period. Audre's courage, her honesty, reminded us that we could not act for ourselves or others if we could not transform our own silence into speech."[22] Lorde recognized how often people in "movements" begin to behave like their oppressors toward one another. Her poetry often echoed the lessons she had learned as an outsider:

> stop killing
> the other
> in ourselves
> the self that we hate in others.[23]

In person, Lorde was an epiphany of the African/Caribbean/ American spirit—colorful, brilliant, full of the power of the erotic, which she reinvented for a culture that had killed it. The daughter of Caribbean immigrants, she grew up in New York City but lived in diverse cultures: Europe, the United States, Mexico. In her last years, she returned to St. Croix and the islands of her foremothers to die.

She was often the only black woman's voice in the early days of the women's movement, and often took on the "heavyweights" with no hesitation. She reimagined and redefined concepts and myths that were buried in the sands of struggle. She forced blacks and whites, activists and theologians, men and women, to remove their colonized glasses and really see. Her essay "The Uses of the Erotic: The Erotic as Power" exceeds anything written in our era in its power to liberate the soul from dualism. She recognized that contemporary society has reduced the erotic to the plastic sensation, a trivial, confused and sometimes pathological experience. The erotic, which is so often used as an instrument of dominance in our culture, has become a gesture of impotence. Lorde restored, in her own life as artist, activist and lover, and in the social consciousness, the sense of the *erotic as power*.

For the erotic is not a question of what we do; it is a question of how acutely and fully we can feel in the doing. Once we know the extent to which we are capable of feeling that sense of satisfaction and completion, we can then observe which of our various life endeavors bring us closest to that fullness.[24]

Lorde epitomized the embodied wisdom of the *subjugated knowledge* that modern civilization, West and East, must relearn. To understand the erotic as she did is to be incapable of equating pornography with eroticism, or to divide the spiritual from the sensual or the personal from the political. "In touch with the erotic, I become less willing to accept powerlessness."

Audre Lorde stood at the intersection of racism, sexism, and homophobia and saw that all three are rooted in the same source, in "the inability to recognize the notion of *difference* as a dynamic human force which is enriching rather than threatening to the defined self."[25]

Women's lives have been different, even when their starting point and goal are perceived to be similar to their male peers. For example, both Teilhard de Chardin and Thomas Merton found pivotal experiences in encounters with the feminine and with the East. Their trajectories were relatively linear and predictable. Both began their search from a religious orientation. Their choice of a social role was singular and varied little over the course of their lives. They expressed their life-learning primarily through thinking and writing.

Joanna Macy—mother, wife, scholar, teacher, activist, writer, and contemplative—began her search from a similar standpoint: firmly rooted in the Judaeo-Christian tradition. Hers was a religious search at the outset. In the years when she was raising her three children she studied religion, first her own Protestant tradition and then Buddhism. At the same time her sensitivity to social justice drew her to political science and the ideas of the Enlightenment, Marxism, the prophets of the 1960s. She worked in the Peace Corps, the State Department, the Urban League, and was a very visible participant in the movements for civil rights, prison reform, safe energy and environment, and peace. She lived for long periods of time in South and Central Asia, Tibet, and India. As Macy remembers, "Back and forth I went between these two poles of life, the spiritual and the political: from meditating to public speaking, from preparing testimony on nuclear waste to reading Sanskrit texts."[26] With each passing year the distance between the poles seemed to grow shorter, until they apparently converged in 1980 in the Sarvodaya movement in Sri Lanka, a Buddhist-inspired self-help movement.

For Joanna Macy, the starting point and goal have always been the same, but the way there has been a zigzag, improvised adventure. For her, religion is the key element in the transformation of society; it provides the vision, the values, and the impetus for change. When it becomes encumbered with the baggage of culture and social constructs, its purpose is muted. But every tradition can tap its own roots "to rearticulate the possibilities of the human spirit."

> To the extent that Marxism, national socialism, or capitalism claims to embody the *summum bonum,* the final perception and fulfillment of life, they too are religious; where they are understood to serve more limited means and are judged by broader or higher standards, these very standards are religious in nature. Of this nature are the final criteria operative in the allocation of resources, time, energy. Whether or not these criteria appear religious, they stem from value-systems—or are re-ordered in the light of value-systems—which, in the last analysis, are articles of faith.[27]

Joanna Macy's search has been for a value system that enhances *connection* and transforms the perception of *difference*. For many years she was drawn to Buddhism and the East before she understood why. She recounts her realization that other religions held similar values of compassion, nonviolence, love, and self-restraint. "Other faiths acknowledged the same kinds of responsibility and service; but in Buddha Dharma these ethical norms had a transparent, unburdened quality. Why, in the Buddhist context, did they feel so accessible, so liberating?"[28] After many years of formal study and Buddhist discipline, Macy realized that the key to her attraction to Buddhism was the core teaching of *paticca samuppada* or the "dependent co-arising of all phenomena." This is often referred to as the Buddhist law of causality, the Dharma.

This core teaching released Macy from Western notions of power and absolute transcendence, and the notions of *difference* that Western religions inspire. Her contemporary, Mary Catherine Bateson, once called the Western religions of Judaism, Christianity, and Islam "a compendium of solutions to encounters with *other* ways of seeing the world," encounters with those who are perceived as the stranger, the outsider. "Abraham's God is a jealous God, and truth is exclusive."[29]

The Buddha Dharma, on the other hand, tolerates no precedence or hierarchy. Causality itself is an interdependent "co-arising." Things do not produce each other or make each other happen, as in linear causality; they *help* each other happen by providing context, occasion, or locus, and in so doing they are affected in a reciprocal dynamic of mutuality. There is relationship and connection, but not power. The teaching of Buddha is grounded in this mutuality, this dynamic at work within the universe. Free of the necessity for supernatural authority, the way of Buddha emphasized the interdependence of all phenomena. Macy explains:

> I saw how it underlay everything he taught about the self, suffering and liberation from suffering. I noted how it knocked down the dichotomies bred by hierarchical thinking, the old polarities between mind and matter, self and world, that had exasperated me as a spiritual seeker and activist, and as a woman. I saw how it brought the Buddha into conflict with the religious beliefs of his day, distancing him from earlier philosophical thought. I saw it as consonant with the systems thinking emerging in our own era, and important to our understanding of this new process paradigm, so that we can develop it with greater fullness and depth. Indeed I felt as if I had come upon an ancient forgotten city, overgrown by jungle and awaiting rediscovery and restoration.[30]

Perhaps this insight also explains the illuminating epiphany that Thomas Merton experienced in his encounter with the Buddha in Polonnaruwa, Sri Lanka, a few weeks before his death. He regarded it as the ultimate clarification and revelation of his Asian pilgrimage. Sri Lanka, for some mysterious reason, provided a key point of light in the lives of both seekers, Macy and Merton. Macy went on to discover more in Sri Lanka.

The Buddhist doctrine of "dependent co-arising" confirmed Macy's lifelong intuitive sense of the interconnectedness of all things and the illusory nature of the Western ego. Many of her teachings and practices, for example, *Despair and Personal Power in the Nuclear Age,* are rooted in this sense of being part of an intricate web of living creatures:

> It has led me to see that even my pain for the world is a function of this mutual belonging, like a cell experiencing the larger body. Because it shows that causality, or power, resides in relationships rather than in persons or institutions, it offers the courage to resist conformity and to act in new ways to change the situation.[31]

This sensitivity places her at the center of an emerging consciousness sometimes referred to as "deep ecology." The perception of the self is key to this perspective, as it is to the Buddhist teaching. She is fond of quoting Gregory Bateson's view that the idea of a reified, skin-encapsulated ego is "the epistemological fallacy of the Occidental civilization."[32] She counters the conventional notion of the ego with a conception of the *ecological self* or the *green self,* which is co-extensive with other beings and the life of the planet. Like others, she sees human beings as cells of a larger organism, the Gaia, the earth-cosmos system that gave us birth. For Joanna Macy *difference* is swallowed up in our essential unity.

Macy recounts several moments of "awakening" she experienced in the Orient. One time she heard a Buddhist nun explaining the underlying principles of the Buddhist teaching on compassion: "So countless are all sentient beings, and so many are their births throughout time, that each at some point was your mother." The idea of viewing each person, every creature, as one's mother changes one's perspective radically. Macy remembers that the next person she saw on the path returning from the school was a load-bearing laborer or coolie, an outsider. At first she looked away in discomfort, as we often do when confronted by someone who is miserably poor or a wretched outcast. Then she was drawn to the bent, weathered figure struggling with a load up the hill. The coolie was no longer an invisible person.

> I wanted to see his face. . . . What face did she now wear, this dear one who had long ago mothered me? . . . I wanted to touch that dark, half-glimpsed cheek, and meet those lidded eyes bent to the ground. . . . Whether out of respect or embarrassment, I did not do that. I simply stood five feet away and drank in every feature of that form—the grizzled chin, the rag turban, the gnarled hands grasping the forward overhang of log. The customary comments of my internal social scientist evaporated. What appeared now before me was not an oppressed class or an indictment of an economic system, so much as a distinct, irreplaceable, and incomparably precious being. My mother. . . . The furnishings of my mind had been rearranged, my heart broken open.[33]

Today, Joanna Macy continues her journey into deeper awareness of what it means to be in connection. In recent correspondence with her I learned that her journey into the heart of Eastern consciousness had a parallel journey as a woman through the contemporary transformations of the feminine consciousness. It has also made a difference in her perspective. She sees her thinking continuing to evolve, "as a spiral." Presently she is focused on "direct diagnosis of the industrial growth society (IGS) and direct action, even 'magic' to dismantle it."[34]

As with other women, Macy's life has been full of surprises and turns in the road, but a common thread of improvisation and innovation runs through all the "seasons." Perhaps it is because she is a woman, carrying the *subjugated knowledge* of the feminine, that her encounter with the East has led to very concrete, practical applications of the interdependence that these ideas inspire.

Her conversion to the Buddhist perspective of "co-arising" and compassion led her eventually to the discovery of the Sarvodaya movement in Sri Lanka. The movement focuses on the empowerment of small villages, gives them a way of identifying their basic needs and local problems, and of solving them together through contributed labor. The word *sarvodaya* means "the awakening of all." In empowering the young as well as the old, ignoring all class lines, blurring gender discrimination, and incorporating religious pluralism, not depending on large accumulations of capital or land, it represents an alternative to the ordinary configurations of power. The movement has a spiritual energy, in that the villagers are continually challenged to become more than they were, in their self-image and in the reconstruction of their interrelations. While rooted in the teachings of Buddhism, its core is a universalism that dissolves partisan community elements and promotes development in the true sense.

There are analogous movements and experiments emerging all over the world: the Village Action movement in Scandinavia, the base communities of Latin America, Australian Landcare communities, and many others. Women and "outsiders" are very active in these new projects that provide an antidote to apathy, powerlessness, and individualism. The atomism and impotence of modern developed societies leave us vulnerable to the loss of one of the basic prerequisites for life: differentiation. Paradoxically, many of these movements that promote a sense of *unity* in action actually do so by capitalizing on difference and diversity.

It is all too easy to forget the crucial importance of *difference* in the maintenance of life itself. The human brain, the immune system, the ecosystem, the planet, and the universe all depend on it. Teilhard de Chardin, the great philosopher of the evolving cosmos, also saw the psychic and spiritual implications:

> A world on the way to concentration of consciousness, you think, would be all joy? On the contrary, I answer. It is just such a world that is the most natural and necessary seat of suffering. . . . A personalizing evolution is necessarily painful: it is basically a plurality; it advances by differentiation; it leads to metamorphoses.[35]

This loss of *difference* in many dimensions of modern existence threatens human and social development. We see it in the commodification and homogenization of culture: through advertising, which reduces our taste and preference to sameness; through the media, which reduces sex to nakedness, intimacy to "letting it all hang out," perception to sound bites, and knowing to the death of the imagination. We see it in the education system. Japan is a case in point:

> Japan presents the spectacle of a thoroughly commodified world of knowledge. . . . The Japanese examination system is a perfect allegory for Japanese late capitalism: the apparatus of the conveyor belt is the machine metaphor for the system which conveys children from good kindergarten to good company—a movement which has absolutely no essential basis, and which reveals, in the guise of a fantasy of security, the actual insecurity of the ceaseless progress of modern societies.[36]

We see the loss of healthy differentiation in the monopolies that capitalism is now generating, where a half-dozen or fewer corporations can control an entire sector of our economy, or where a Wal-Mart will cause the demise of local businesses. We see the phenomenon of computerization dissolving privacy and producing "groupthink." We see the dogmatism of a postmodern Catholic Church trying to recreate the Holy Roman Empire and claiming infallibility. In many parts of the world, imperialism still holds many people hostage. While twentieth-century technology has benefitted us immeasureably, we are beginning to see the cost, including its inevitable effect of driving out the competition, excluding the alternative.

While visiting Japan I heard of a Japanese woman, an environmental activist, who has been a voice crying in the wilderness about an issue that has terrible implications for the future. She discovered that the two biggest Japanese seed companies have patented a range of seeds produced in their laboratories and have gained exclusive government contracts that give them a virtual monopoly over the kind of food that will be grown in Japan. In a "green" journalism article, she notes,

> The new seeds are the result of genetic engineering by scientists, aiming at breeding only the strains that produce the biggest crop— even though these strains may in fact be too weak and specialized to

survive if, for example, any severe climactic change should be placed upon them. They also have no relevance to the local land on which they will be grown—so by using them our society is getting rid of the whole notion of producing food suited to local conditions and which is organically diverse. Food is being turned, from something on which we know we can always subsist in our local communities, into a massive centralized industry.[37]

This new awareness was compounded when I returned home to the United States and discovered that a large transnational corporation, W. R. Grace, has become involved in patenting engineered seeds! Monopoly, standardization, exclusive rights, sameness threaten to destroy us and our planet. As Macy puts it, "Uniformity is entropic, the kiss of death."[38]

Perhaps the most visible reminder of the importance of *difference* and *differentiation* is the growing evidence of a diminishing biodiversity on our planet. Each day thousands of species are disappearing—plants, animals, birds, fish, insects. The shrinking of the rainforests threatens not only this diversity but the fuel of life itself: oxygen.

Toward the end of my visit to Japan I was riding the bullet train from Hiroshima back to Nagoya and musing on how such trains might significantly reduce CFCs, ozone inversions, and auto congestion in the United States. Millions of people ride the trains in Japan—the stations and terminals are omnipresent and the hordes that crowd onto them are unbelievable. I noticed that almost everyone on my train had a box lunch or breakfast. At the next stop I saw hundreds of people lined up at kiosks to buy their carry-along food. At every stop along the way I saw the same thing—the box lunches were sold on the train, on the platforms, in the terminals. I started calculating, because each box—top and bottom—was made entirely of wood. And I saw the empty ones hauled away with the garbage, evidently with no plan for recycling. Then I thought of all the chopsticks, and calculated again. Now I understood why the Malaysian rainforests were disappearing.

Then I thought of the Amazon and the developers, Alaska and the timber industry in North America, and the rape of wilderness

everywhere—the loss of all that biodiversity, with its secrets of healing plants and breathing trees and species whose importance to the
existence of our "blue planet" we do not even know. Riding along
in the train I felt the sudden urge to weep. Despair would be a natural response to the enormity of the problem and the seeming
impossibility of solving it in the face of unchecked vested interests.
Then I remembered the response of John Seed when Joanna Macy
asked him how he managed to overcome his despair in the face of
the timber predators: "I try to remember that it's not me, John
Seed, trying to protect the rainforest. Rather I am part of the rainforest protecting myself, I am that part of the rainforest recently
emerged into human thinking."[39]

My first visit to the East and the days I spent in Japan—where conformity and homogeneity are the norm—stirred me to many reflections on *diversity* as well as *difference.* I felt gratitude for all that
still survives and all that annoys us, all that prods us toward transformation. I also felt an urgency to reclaim the wonderful legacy of
the outsiders, the minority voices, the marginated ones of history—
especially women. Because their experience has been different,
perhaps because they have a stronger sense of connection with all
living things, they can make a difference for our future. *Difference,
diversity,* these are precious spiritual and material resources, the
womb of the *subjugated knowledges* that will enable us to survive,
evolve, and flourish.

In our personal lives, in the life of the culture and the planet, the
encounter with *difference* will be either the chief obstacle or the
primary catalyst of growth—of our capacity to learn from this wisdom and use it to shape a new paradigm. Competition can drown
out the curiosity that *difference* should excite. Fear and the retreat
to fundamentalism can stifle the corrective feedback that will preserve our best values in the midst of change. Addictions of all kinds
can numb us so that we do not have to feel *difference*, and therefore, do not have to grow. The choice is ours.

House of Gold
Heron nests nearby.
Crimson carp
Timelessness.

Beauty.
Nude painting
Blossoms wait to be enjoyed.
Longing to leave
The frame.

Visitors.
Magic scarabs
Seek the light
Exit.

Rose
Unfolding in the night.
Morning, memory
Ghost of love.

Chapter Six

In Search of Eve and Our True Mother

Within hours after my arrival in Japan I met her for the first time. Passing a shrine on the way into Nara, I saw the figure in the dim shadows, her devotees gathering around her. First they clapped their hands three times, then bowed reverently and remained in that posture of prayer for several minutes. At the time I wasn't sure if the effigy in the shrine was a male or a female god; it made me curious to know more.

Toward the end of my conversation with the High Priest of Kofukugi Temple on my first day in Japan, the Reverend Tagawa offered me a beautiful gift—an autographed copy of a book he has written on Kannon, the Goddess of Mercy. This was the second of many encounters with Kannon, perhaps the most omnipresent deity in Japanese life. I saw her everywhere: in temples and street shrines, in homes and harbors, in train stations and gift shops, even in gas stations. Who was this mysterious, magnetic icon that attracted so much respect and trust and supplication?

I happened to be in Nara during a holiday when Japanese honor Prince Shotoku, a kind of Jesus-figure who established Buddhism in Japan. One of the most impressive temple areas, Horyjugi in Nara, is a complex of magnificent buildings founded by Prince Shotoku in the early seventh century. It is a treasure house of sculptures, icons, painting, and all sorts of decorative arts. It is a popular place of pilgrimage, and here, once again, I encountered some of the most stunning images of Kannon—always surrounded by

110

crowds of praying pilgrims. The seven-foot, slender, almost modernistic Kudara Kannon was hypnotizing—all the more mysterious because it supposedly came from Korea. In Japan, Kannon functions as the goddess of mercy and childbirth. Clearly she has a connection with ancient fertility cults. She is often depicted with many eyes and many arms, signifying her omniscient eyes of compassion and her infinite resources of help.

At Horyjugi I learned of the popular Japanese belief that Prince Shotoku was actually a manifestation of Kannon who appeared in Japan to bring salvation to the Japanese people. Kannon it seems, was an immigrant—a Far Eastern reincarnation of the Near Eastern, Indian god Avalokiteshvara, a male deity regarded as an incarnation of Buddha.

By now, my interest in Kannon had become a quest. This was a peripatetic goddess, and one whose gender had been transformed more than once by folk religion as she moved eastward. Why? Buddhist sculpture often expresses a certain sexual ambivalence or androgyny—perhaps suggesting "a femininity which seems to have been freed from the battle of the sexes."[1] What was the significance of the transformation into the feminine?

Kannon's male predecessor, Avalokiteshvara, was clearly associated with the compassion of Buddha. His name is often translated "He Who Hears the Outcries of the World." There are more than thirty different representations of the god, distinguished by the number of heads and arms as well as by the attributes held in the hands. The god of a thousand eyes, a thousand arms, and eleven faces is symbolic of the universal, infinite aspect of his compassion. According to the Indian legend, as the god Avalokiteshvara looked down on the suffering of the world, his head literally burst from pain. His spiritual father reassembled the pieces as eleven new heads. The wish to help all beings caused him to grow 1,000 arms, with an eye in the palm of each. The 1,001 statues of Kannon that I saw in the great Sanjusangen-do Hall in Kyoto carry out this same symbolism.

In China a transformed Avalokiteshvara is venerated as Kuan-Yin or Guanyin. In early times, until the beginning of the Sung Dynasty,

Kuan-Yin was depicted as a male—sometimes even with a moustache. By the tenth century the physical traits of Kuan-Yin were decidedly feminine. Some believe this was the effect of Taoist and Tantric influence, but many historians believe the image was overlaid on the earlier, more indigenous myth of Nu Kua, the creatrix who patched the fragmented cosmos together. Thus images of Kuan-Yin riding on a dolphin may be related to the fish-tailed images of Nu Kua.[2]

Kuan-Yin is always portrayed in Chinese folk legend as one who chose not to be married. Today she is unquestionably the most popular deity that survives in China; her image is found in family altars as well as in temples and monasteries, where she is often a central figure. The female goddess has achieved a status equal in the popular mind to that of the male Buddha. For some Chinese she is even more important.

In Japan, as in other Asian countries, Kannon and her various incarnations are usually referred to as "Buddhas of Mercy." Who was the ancestor of the peripatetic goddess? Her origin seems to have been in the Middle East, most likely Sumerian Iran; perhaps even earlier in Africa. In any case the archetype of the Great Mother traveled from the Middle East to India, then to Tibet. From Tibet she undoubtedly passed over the Silk Road to China, then to Korea, and finally to Japan.

Shun'ei Tagawa believes the most recent change in gender began in China. There, the god was gradually transformed from male to asexual to female. The change reflects a cultural projection. He speculates that it is related to the perceived symbolism of the masculine and feminine consciousness. The masculine consciousness tends to be exclusionary; it creates a hierarchy of value between good/evil, beauty/ugliness, superior/inferior. The masculine consciousness is one-sided; it rejects the "other." In contrast, the feminine consciousness erases hierarchy; it is more inclusive. All things are valued as part of a whole; value is relative, nothing is devalued as ugly or inferior or evil.

Tagawa speaks of this consciousness as a kind of "mothering way of seeing reality."[3] "Kannon's way," he says, is very much needed in a human condition that is mixed with so much *difference*. It must be added that ultimately, in the Rev. Tagawa's mind, the significance of Kannon's gender is irrelevant: "Kannon is beyond gender," because in his view gender is merely a human perspective projected on a divine energy. But "Kannon's Way" teaches that everything must be accepted as a part of a larger whole that we cannot see or understand clearly. We must learn how to understand and act with the compassion, the empathy, and understanding of the great Mother of All.

Lately I have become more aware of the multiform manifestations of the goddess that seem to be emerging in our era. In my youth, goddesses were chiefly Greek and Roman effigies that gathered dust in textbooks or museums. The only experience I had of a goddess was Mary, the Mother of Jesus, who retained a very powerful presence in the Catholic religion. She was indeed a goddess, omnipresent and the object of worship as well as of intense supplication—but we could never admit it. Culture continued to thrive on her image even while rational authority denied its significance. Catholic reality was muted by a Catholic theology that had room for only one God, and a male one at that. The more "education" I received the more the image of the Great Mother receded in my consciousness.

But the peripatetic goddess met me, surprised me at many crossroads. In Latin America I was awed by the living presence of the Pacha Mama in the minds of the indigenous people. Even when the conquering Spaniards sought to obliterate her memory and traditions, she remained deeply rooted in the people. I saw the devotion, the homage paid to her among the Andeans, in their marketplaces, in their fields, on their animals, in their art, in their "Catholic" rituals.

I met the goddess again in Ireland. The first time it was in Trinity College when I saw the images of Mary in the Book of Kells. When these images were juxtaposed with earlier images of the Great Mother from Celtic or megalithic times, the resemblance was startling. My second encounter with the goddess in Ireland was even more of a revelation.

In June of 1995, on my way from Dublin to the West Coast of Ireland, I visited the famous passage grave at Newgrange. Although I had seen pictures of the great passage tomb, I was unprepared for its actual size. The huge mound of soil and stone, with its grassy overlay, was a stunning icon of the belly of a pregnant Mother Earth. As I descended into the dark, narrow passageway to the central burial area, my shoulders rubbed along the sides of the passageway, and I thought of my mother's birthing struggle with her children—she often remarked about our "broad shoulders" and the difficulty they caused in the birth canal.

Descending into the six-thousand-year-old tomb, I felt as though I was reliving my birth, in reverse. Stepping into the circular burial chamber deep in the bowels of the earth, I realized that the women historians were right; this was more than a tomb or a "solar clock." These explanations by earlier historians (all male) shrunk into insignificance in the actual presence of Newgrange. Any structure so profound is usually made to honor deity. I was sure that the people of the early megalithic cultures had designed these magnificent structures to honor death as a ritual of rebirth into Mother Earth, a return to the Mother of All. As one philosopher has said, what myth could be more fundamental and powerful for the human species than birth and the experience of the womb: "it is the oldest event that forms the matrix and prototypical pattern of human life."[4] There are remnants of many similar tombs throughout Ireland and Western Europe. There are mound constructions in North America that seem to have a similar connection with a female deity. The Great Mother has left her footprints everywhere.

In the 1970s during a trip to Spain I met the Black Madonna for the first time at Montserrat, one of the most ancient sites of Christian mysticism in the Western world. Framed by the stunning mountainous landscape, her image has attracted pilgrims for centuries. As with the goddess Kannon, the encounter was the beginning of a spiritual exploration that continues to this day. Last year I traveled to Montserrat again and revisited the Black Madonna. The shrine was more crowded and busier than it had been in 1971. I had a long wait as the line curled up around the basilica from the plaza, and when I got to the statue, I had barely a moment to glimpse her face before being told to move on quickly.

When I returned to the main foyer of the basilica, a service was about to begin. A tiny priest dressed in black was in the sanctuary pulpit, preaching about the "Our Father." He was dwarfed by the crowds passing behind and above him, absorbed in their devotion, attention focused on the "Great Mother" in the brightly lit niche above the sanctuary. That vignette is etched so clearly in my memory, for it seemed to be a prophetic icon, a reminder of our true spiritual ancestry: there was the golden goddess with the black face transcending time and the brief moment of patriarchy, with its worship of the male and the little white-faced priests in their black robes. In that moment I said aloud, "The people are more attached to her than to his 'Father-God'—this is their true spiritual ground."

There are several Black Madonnas or Black Virgins throughout Europe. Theirs are among the most venerated shrines in the world. Historians believe these statues were brought back to Europe as booty from the Crusades, but the images have their origins in the cults of Isis, Cybele, and Artemis. The statues were often placed near wells or sites of ancient pre-Christian goddesses. Gradually the mythology of the Virgin Mary displaced the memorials of the pre-Christian Great Mother. But the blackness of these goddesses betrays their true ancestry: black was the alchemical color of Wisdom—the black stone of Cybele, the black veil of Isis, the black robe of the exiled Shekinah, the black images of Demeter and Artemis.

One of the most profound revelations of the multiform Great Mother-Goddess has been the rediscovery of her identity as Sophia/Wisdom. One who embarks on the spiritual journey will inevitably encounter her. The early formulators of the Christian tradition were, for the most part, bent on displacing the pagan Great Mother with an Almighty Father and his Son. Baring and Cashford describe the disappearance:

> The Old Testament image of Sophia as the consort of Yahweh and as the craftswoman of creation, who is also "active in the world" as a guiding presence and intelligence within all appearances, vanishes

in the early centuries of the Christian era, as does the Gnostic image of Sophia as consort of the deity and the "womb" of creation. In the Gnostic myth, the ancient connection is retained, however obscurely, between the mother goddess, as Sophia, and Christ, her son, who is sent by the Mother-Father Source to rescue their daughter.[5]

The loss of the image of a goddess as a living spiritual reality undoubtedly had much to do with the translation of Wisdom/ Sophia from a feminine to a masculine image. The conversion began in the Old Testament and in the evolution of Mediterranean languages. The Greek and Latin words for wisdom, like the Hebrew word, have the feminine gender, but in English the word "wisdom" carries no associations with either gender. "It becomes simply an abstract noun rather than an image of the archetypal feminine."[6]

Theologians Elisabeth Schüssler Fiorenza and Elizabeth Johnson have researched and written extensively about this transposition in the Christian tradition, especially in works such as Schüssler Fiorenza's *In Memory of Her* and *Jesus: Miriam's Child, Sophia's Prophet;* and Johnson's *She Who Is.* As Western Christianity developed the mother goddess was eclipsed; Jesus becomes the only son of a father god and a lowly human mother, and acquires the qualities that once belonged to Sophia. Jesus is incarnated as Logos, the word, a distinctly masculine concept. The impact of this displacement on the development of Western spirituality has been all-encompassing. Elaine Pagels observes:

> By the time the process of sorting the various writings ended—probably as late as the year 200—virtually all the feminine imagery for God had disappeared from orthodox Christian tradition.[7]

Consequently, in the West we see so many of the female gods of antiquity displaced, devalued, distorted into evil symbols, fragmented and castrated, transformed into monsters and witches. The stories of Inanna, Tiamat, Demeter, and so many others mirror the primordial loss. In hindsight, these goddess/archetypes seem to be manifestations of the Great Mother, and Eve a pale shadow of the primal feminine.

> In Sophia's exile we can see Eve's expulsion from the garden of Eden, and suddenly this older myth can be read as a story of consciousness losing the memory of its "home" as it leaves the paradise of the Garden. Similarly, in the fairy tales of Sleeping Beauty and Snow White the Gnostic myth gleams through every word, even to the hedge of thorns that stands between the prince and princess, and Snow White lying asleep in her glass coffin.[8]

Eve took the place of First Mother and cast a diminished, subjugated, and guilty shadow on her human progeny. Anthropologists associate this new myth of creation with the Iron Age. It symbolizes a loss of unity and harmony with the divine and a new condition of separation and estrangement. God is now remote and distant from creation; nature is flawed and subject to domination. The transformation is embedded in the language of the myth, in the very name of Eve. Her name, *Hawwah,* and the name *Yahweh* are derived from the same root, a Hebrew verb meaning *to be*. Her power is further compromised by the inversion and pejoration of the symbols of the Serpent and the Tree of Life. When associated with the ancient goddesses, serpents were symbols of their power, their prophetic gifts, and life-giving creative energy. In the Eve myth the associations are inverted and demonized. Eve is punished for desiring *experience*, for wanting to *know* and *taste*.

The dissociation of the Tree of Knowledge from the Tree of Life denigrates embodied experience and injects a degenerate dualistic principle into the tradition, from which we still struggle to be free today. Eve's expulsion was the denial of embodied knowledge and the exaltation of abstract principle. The story of the Fall begins as a myth reflecting a new consciousness and ends as a doctrine reinforcing the new patriarchal order. In the new order suffering and death are punishments for sin, and all of nature is in bondage. The "necessary fault" ushers in mortality and linear time. Like Inanna, Eve is stripped of her royal prerogatives; her powerful gifts are taken from her, and she is left to wither on the sands of time as temptress and fool, willful and lacking in self-control, inferior to man, the "devil's gateway," scapegoat.

As Eve became the central archetype of the subjugated, denigrated feminine, Sophia disappeared into the mystical traditions of both Christianity and Judaism. In Christianity she reappeared sometimes as Wisdom, but more often her attributes were associated with Jesus, then with Mary in later centuries. In Judaism, she appeared as the Shekinah, chiefly in Kabbalistic writings. One of her most remarkable reappearances was in the visions and writings of the mystic Hildegard in the eleventh century. Barbara Newman, a Hildegard scholar, believes she is the first Christian thinker to incorporate the ancient archetypal feminine in a serious and systematic way in her work. Not only did Hildegard formulate her thoughts within the traditional framework of Christian symbolism through the feminine archetypes of Eve, Mary, Ecclesia, Synogoga, and women saints like Ursula, but her own mystical visions and lyrical compositions are suffused with the numinous figure that is at the heart of her spiritual world, a figure she calls Sapientia or Caritas. Newman claims that these images transcend allegory and attain the stature of theophany.[9] After Hildegard's death, the archetypal feminine was reduced to being a handmaid of the profoundly masculinized theology and imagery of the Christian tradition. Like solitary voices in the wilderness, an occasional mystic resurrected the feminine face of God.

Now these ancestor archetypes are rising from the ashes of time, surfacing in human consciousness again. Today, the archetypal feminine seems to be bursting out everywhere. Books on the goddess fill the bookstores; women scholars conduct fascinating explorations of the ancient sites of the goddess, spirituality groups multiply—exploring the "goddess within" and shaping a feminine spirituality. Even the traditional churches are being dragged kicking and screaming into re-imagining their traditions with a feminine face. These powerful and numinous figures are appearing not only in the research of historians and anthropologists, in theological scholarship and spiritual reflections, but even in our dreams.

Perhaps the most powerful evidence that these archetypes are emerging for a purpose is revealed in the process of psychotherapy. As a therapist I have seen many women and men in whom the feminine is either buried or struggling to emerge. I have been amazed and awed at the frequency that archetypal images of the feminine— sometimes in the form of powerful female figures, sometimes in symbolic images clearly related to the feminine—are surfacing in the sleep dreams as well as the lucid dreams—the daylight imaginings—of my clients. I find other women, and some men, who experience these same archetypal elements popping up, even when not intentionally working with the unconscious. When the images are female figures, they are usually powerful but "with kind eyes, and strong arms"; sometimes they are amazon-like in appearance, sometimes dark and fearsome like Kali. Sometimes they are surrounded by nature or animals, like Native American mythic figures. These latter female archetypes are especially surprising, since they are emerging from the unconscious of Euro-Americans or Afro-Americans. Perhaps beyond the collective unconscious there is also an unconscious filled with the "spirits of the place," as in the Japanese experience.

This eruption of the feminine in some who may be in the early stages of "coming awake"— most frequently women past thirty-five, or men in an identity crisis—is counterpointed by the mummified condition of the feminine in many younger women and men. From age ten or so on, women in the Western developed world undergo a progressive disempowerment that represses, devalues, ignores, and denigrates the feminine. The cost of competence in society for the American woman who pursues work or a career is a denial of female-identification and an overidentification with males, male values, and male-identified ways. They must play stereotypical female roles at home and in intimate relations; they must be like men at work. Self-esteem and self-confidence often plummet; role models that would image *difference* are scarce; women's ways of knowing and doing are repressed; feminine energy and creativity are hypnotized and starve for lack of nourishment. For young males the cost of being male is the denial of the feminine and the consequent vulnerability to dependency when they seek women as a proxy for the feeling life that has been so crippled.[10]

So there has been a great repression in the souls of modern women and men and a cultural amnesia from which some are struggling to awake. The struggle is recorded in the deepest recesses of consciousness and mirrors a struggle recorded in many myths.

One myth that is particularly meaningful for the subjugated consciousness today—whether in women, men, or others who have suffered in some way from social repression—is the ancient story of Inanna. In the ancient world of the Mideast, the Great Mother-Goddess was worshiped under many names: Ishtar, Astarte, Ahanita, Ma, and Asherah. But she was probably first known as Inanna, a deity of ancient Sumer, a land between the Tigris and the Euphrates rivers, sometimes referred to as the cradle of civilization, the southern part of modern Iraq. The myth, a compilation of older myths in a narrative poem called *Hymn to Inanna,* records the story of the great Goddess-queen who prevailed until the time of the Great Reversal (around 3500 B.C.E.) when the growth of city-states, class-structured society, greed for land, slavery, and competition ushered in the patriarchal order.

At the peak of her worldly and shamanic powers, Inanna consummates a sacred marriage with a shepherd. The marriage represents the merging of pastoral and agricultural civilizations and the beginning of a transition to patriarchy. Like many mythic heroes, Inanna undertakes a journey to the Underworld, where she is stripped of all her power and where she encounters her dark sister, Ereshkigal. To see Ereshkigal is to die. She is the one who has been abandoned, sacrificed, raped, wounded. She is full of rage, envy, hunger, loneliness. In the original myth Ereshkigal is a former grain/fertility goddess banished to the Underworld apparently because she represents what is antithetical to patriarchal values of rationalized control. Thus the dark sister is in reality the power of Inanna, muted and mutilated by the new order.

Inanna is powerless, abandoned to death. But her spiritual alter-ego, a confidante and priestess, intercedes on her behalf. Inanna returns only to find that her consort has usurped her powers and prerogatives. Inanna has returned wiser than before. She punishes her consort by insisting that he make a journey to the Underworld and forges a compromise that will insure the death and rebirth of the earth and its life-giving cycles each year. Her partner must learn, as she has, to balance wisdom with power, honor death as well as life, to balance *yin* and *yang* in the exercise of leadership.

The myth of Inanna mirrors a journey that many women and other disempowered people must make to salvage their own sanity and social power. A remarkable story of this same journey is recorded in the paintings and reflections of Tataya Mato in her book *The Black Madonna Within*.[11] Mato is a German survivor of the terrors of childhood abuse as well as the horrors of the Russian front during World War II. The archetype of the Black Madonna emerged out of her own dreams during her healing process many years later. It is clearly an amalgam of the "dark sister," which has been repressed, Mato's personal shadow, and the life-giving, nurturing powers from the "ground beneath." Ultimately the archetype of the Black Madonna becomes a "spirit guide" for her journey through life, but also an image of her healed, whole self.

Three other goddess-archetypes appear later in her process: Sophia-Shekinah, Kwan Yin (Kannon), and White Buffalo Woman. The quartet is reminiscent of Toni Wolff's redefinition of women's inner psychology in terms of feminine archetypes. Wolff rebelled against the "colonization" of woman's inner life by images and language derived from male experience. Wolff describes the mother, hetaira, amazon, and medial (wise) woman archetypes as inherent in all women. Archetypes, as defined in our first chapter, are traces of crystallized experience that are stored in the collective unconscious, possibly transmitted in genetic memory. They are energy "transformers" that have the power to constellate new experience.

Mato's four archetypes come out of her active imagination as well as her unconscious and carry a meaning and message: The Black Madonna is the medial energy that impels us to communicate with our own unconscious, the repressed and wounded feminine, and the Shadow that is made up of all the pieces of *difference* that we have rejected. Shekinah is the wisdom energy that recalls us to embodied knowledge and activates the imagination, giving birth to an enlightened consciousness and vision for the future. Kwan Yin (Kannon) is the energy of mothering and giving birth, a heart full of compassion and power to nurture and love unconditionally and inclusively. White Buffalo Woman, the shaman of the Sacred Pipe, brings the energy of awareness of our interdependence as creatures, of ourselves as cells in the body of our Great Mother, the Earth/Cosmos. She brings the gift of peace.

In a multiplicity of forms, these dream archetypes and imaginative apparitions are erupting like volcanos of energy that have been asleep for aeons. The phenomenon seems to be universal. Certainly in the East, the eclipse of the feminine has also been recorded in myth, but the goddesses seem to have been able to reclaim their power and restore the balance of feminine/masculine energies—at least in terms of spiritual significance. What of the social impact? These powerful image/energies not only mirror but can help to create a new social order. Symbol goes before and seeds the coming transformation. The recent Fourth World Conference on Women, which drew thirty-thousand women to Beijing—the heart of patriarchal repression of the feminine and of femicide—is a dramatic instance of the power these energies from within, and from below, have to shape the politics and events of our time. In Tiananmen Square it was the image of a goddess that burst forth as a symbol of resistance to tyranny and repression.

Likewise, some believe that the acceleration of visions and apparitions of the Virgin Mary in recent years may also be related to the "theophany" of the feminine. Michael Grosso sees the phenomenon as evidence of a collective unconscious that is catalyzing a spiritual transformation. In a recent interview he comments:

> Marian visions are indeed increasing because the feminine aspect of psychic function is needed at this point in our evolution. She is a completing principle, one that balances the one-sided masculine. . . . She is a sly deconstruction of the patriarchy.[12]

In North America one group of men seems to be particularly sensitive and awake to the sound of the Mother's voice. Native Americans have preserved the connection with the Mother longer than most cultures. Russell Means, a Native American leader and contemporary warrior for justice, disputes the image of the Native American as the brutal savage painted in the folklore of the New World. In an interview he says:

> Understanding that the easiest thing to do in life is kill, it was a dishonor to kill. . . . We didn't go around torturing, maiming and killing white people—unless we suffered such horrendous atrocities that our rage knew no bounds. . . . Our societies are matriarchal—ruled by mothers, and mothers never want to kill babies or anything that's living. When you understand matriarchal societies, you can understand life itself because women create. Women create and give birth. . . . Just think of that. It's awesome, mind-boggling. I can't conceive of that, no male can. They're the only living beings on Earth purified naturally by the universe, in exact time with the moon. How can God be a male entity? . . . Look at these man-made religions, man-made, man-thought-up, man-created religions with a deity that's a man. I don't care if you're a Buddhist, a Hindu, a Jew, Moslem or Christian, every one of those religions justifies imperialism and male supremacy in the name of its male gods. It's scary. This world won't recognize women.[13]

Means goes on to interpret the true significance of the Sioux Sun Dance, the ancient initiation rite for males. Means explains that the whole ceremony was a purification rite to bring the male into balance with the female, to initiate him into the understanding of the woman's strength in bearing suffering, and a spiritual understanding of childbirth. Unfortunately, as Means explains, today many young Indian men and women have been contaminated by the surrounding culture, and they think the Sun Dance is a macho ceremony to show how tough males are.

In spite of the reversals of time and history—this *subjugated knowledge*, the wisdom of the Great Mother—is making itself known. Most of all these apparitions and revisionings are telling us how to be whole, individually and collectively. In simple terms, the recovery of this wholeness is the recovery of *soul*. The artificial and mechanical divisions we have created between certain values and experiences have left us fragmented and deluded creatures. For example:

Life and Death Are One: We, however, have created a society that kills life and avoids or tries to cancel death. Western medicine has been constructed on the premise that suffering and death are evil and must be eliminated. Illness is an "unnatural" state; therefore it must be removed. Thus our healing methods are invasive, mutilating, and impersonal. Particularly in the case of mental illness, elimination is the goal—therefore medication, rather than spiritual integration, is often the first response. Jack Kevorkian is seen as a kind of vampire, rather than as a midwife.

In this respect my own discovery of different approaches to psychotherapy in Japan proved to be illuminating. Western style psychotherapy is not popular in Japan, but in times of particular crisis, some form of intervention becomes necessary. The theory and practice of Morita therapy, for example, emphasize the changing of the inner subjective attitude, whereas in the West we emphasize activity directed toward changing objective reality, through medication or complete withdrawal of symptoms. One practitioner who attempted to introduce Morita therapy in East Germany found that Germans want to be cured of their symptoms and do not want to be told to accept their condition as if it were eternal. "It is almost as if they desired to walk away from their symptoms, as if symptoms were external and detachable things, rather than changing their attitude toward something that is a part of them, part of reality." [14]

Time, Space, and Matter Are One: We know this intellectually if we are current with the new physics, but we persist in dividing life and the universe into linear packages that serve our immediate interests. Culturally, one type of consciousness is focused on the past, trying to recover a lost sense of identity, nationalism or racial esteem, or land once possessed. Another type of consciousness lives in the future, always expecting, working for a time when things will be better or when one may have accumulated more, when "progress" will be achieved. Each consciousness obliterates the present moment—its reality, its challenges, opportunities, joys— and each succumbs to depression, frustration, and rage. Each consciousness forgets that linear time, thrown forward or backward, is a fiction we have devised to deal with the incomprehensibility of ourselves suspended in eternity, the only reality. Perhaps the only phenomena in the modern world that capture "real time" in contrast to linear, fictional time are found in "primitive" tribal societies and in the communal rituals of some religious traditions.

Knowledge and Sensing Are One: Our modern civilization, however, has been constructed for the most part by separating these experiences. Our philosophy, our science, our educational systems, our laws, even our religions are fundamentally abstract. The recovery of *embodied knowledge* means the recovery of our own and others' subjugated experience, and the truth and wisdom that emerges in our own voice. Contemporary feminists and people of color have exposed the dualism inherent in the epistemologies of the dominant culture and are reshaping our perspectives in science, religion, history, political science—all of the rational systems of thought that we have inherited, as well as the creative arts. "Women's Ways of Knowing" are reconnecting the mind-body circuits of our experience and its meaning.

Nature and Human Consciousness Are One: For so many centuries we have thought of humans—ourselves—as the apex of the universe, that all other species and condensations of light (matter) were inferior to this final evolutionary product of human consciousness. Today we are gaining a new perspective; we are beginning to see that consciousness inheres in every particle, every creature of the cosmos and the earth system. We are only a part of the whole that has most recently reached consciousness, and we are only beginning to learn to communicate with other dimensions of conscious activity in the cosmos.

Either/Or Is Really Both/And: Culturally conditioned consciousness has its own logic. And between East and West there are distinct patterns of thinking that are significant. In the West our consciousness is firmly immured in a system of binary logic: a thing either *is*, or it *is not*. Something cannot be and not be at the same time; truth excludes its opposite. Westerners are born into a Cartesian disposition, which is reinforced by all of our institutions. Whereas, frequently in the Orient, paradoxical logic rather than binary logic prevails; perspectives are fluid and multiple. Contradictory things can be simultaneously true. Ambiguity need not be reduced to or resolved by "one over the other." These differences often result in radically different epistemologies or frameworks for thinking. The *Both/And* framework appears to be a functional corrective for a culture that must encompass great diversity and at the same time create a sustainable society.

You and I Are One: All of the great spiritual traditions lead us to this awareness. Whether it is the great teaching of Christian love or Buddhist teaching of compassion and the realization that "all beings at some time have been my mother," the summit of all spiritual perfection lies in the vision of all creatures as cells of one Body, of the One.

Thus, the capacity to hold opposites in tension, whether in the consciousness or in one's experience, has been a mark of spiritual maturity and psychological health in both Western and Eastern traditions. Now it seems that there may also be an analogous cultural imperative. I have seen this development in my own spiritual journey as well as in the belief systems of my clients and significant others. Spiritually–in people who are *becoming souls*–I see this pattern:

In *childhood and youth*, I think we are natural pantheists, unless we are relationally and environmentally deprived. We are sensitive to the spiritual all around us and in us. We respond to the numinous. Later as socialization and education take hold of us, I think we become little fundamentalists, even Calvinists: full of the sense of the divisions between good and evil, sin and virtue, body and mind, safety and danger. The ethical sense keeps pace with the developing conceptual ability, much as Piaget imagined it. We are rather literal minded and focused on living by the rules, or on flaunting them.

In *adulthood* I think most of us become existentialists; religion becomes an overlay. The developing ego is crucial to this phase as is relational experience; but it is also a time when the transcendent meaning of the Bible or the Koran plants in some young adults a strong sense of justice and/or righteousness, and a need of belonging in order to defend ourselves against conflict—both in ourselves and "out there." We respond with zeal to "save" others, and/or we respond with empathy to the pain of the world and experience a call to transform the social order.

Somewhere between *adulthood* and the *second half of life*, if we are faithful to the journey, we make our descent to our own underworld. When we emerge, we are changed. We become more like Buddhists, and eventually more like Buddhists who have been influenced by Taoism. We are no longer compulsively seeking perfection or purity; we no longer harbor illusions about transforming the world tomorrow. So we learn to live more in the present. Compassion and patience are the great virtues; we feel our connection with all beings and are more practiced in the discipline of detachment and letting go; and—most of all—we are able to receive and hold many opposites, differences, all at once. We are more comfortable with contradictions and paradox in ourselves, in others, in events. We have acquired a tolerance for ambiguity. We do not become amnesiacs, but we learn to live with a forgiving memory.

Two of the world's most enduring spiritual philosophies describe this path to the same goal: spiritual perfection lies above all in the capacity to "hold opposites in tension." This is the process described in the iconology of the Zen Buddhist Ox-Herding Pictures. Ten pictures graphically portray the spiritual journey in allegorical terms: from the beginning of the search through the struggle to the silence of the ego, through emptiness and the void to the realization that "everything is Buddha," all is One. The tenth picture, the final icon, "Entering the City With Helping Hands," describes the pilgrim coming full circle, now a purified soul through whom all things can flow.

The Zen-Buddhist philosopher Suzuki describes this final state as a balance: the pilgrim exists in the in-between spaces, suspended from a sense of personal importance but knowing she can be an instrument for others; neither aloof, nor weighed down with responsibility; not so detached that he is absent from life, but not seeking to control it either; a conduit for harmony in the universe.[15]

There are many similar paradigms and paths traced in Western spiritualities. Perhaps the most dramatic parallel is found in Jung's *Mysterium Coniunctionis,*[16] in another series of ten pictures called the *Rosarium philosophorum*, which Jung describes as an alchemical iconology of spiritual individuation. The pictures trace the pilgrim's journey through the emergence of opposites, the stripping and descent, through death and purification by "earth, air, fire, and water," to a final integration in which polarities are suspended. In the *tension of opposites* lies the mystery of spiritual fulfillment. Jung's *Mysterium* seems very close to the theological meaning of the crucifixion of Jesus Christ and the central ambiguity of suffering in the Christian tradition.

As a psychotherapist, I find that when a client has progressed to the point of being able to sustain a *tension of opposites,* a tolerance for ambiguity and polarity in themselves, in others, in the events that happen, in the larger destiny of the world, then I know they have engaged integration, healing, and wholeness.

Whatever is rejected, excluded, or despised in our consciousness—there is where our path to enlightenment lies. So it was with the great spiritual leaders of our civilization—Lao Tzu, Buddha, Jesus, Gandhi, Muhammad—throwing away fortunes and power, consorting with outcasts, espousing unpopular views, surprising our usual ways of thinking. The Taoists in particular seem to have grasped conceptually the inexorable movement of spirit toward a balance of opposites, toward a unity encompassing *difference.* Some have speculated that this may be evidence of the connection with the repressed feminine principle:

> A careful reading of the most basic book of Taoism, the Tao Te Ching . . . may be the mirror in which, to some extent, we are able to observe reflections of ideas and beliefs that may once have been the theological/philosophical core of ancient Goddess reverence in China.[17]

It is difficult to define *Tao* in a Western language. We have no word that is as all-encompassing, yet as subtle. It is made up of two Chinese characters, the symbol for consciousness ("head") and the symbol for "going" or traveling a way. It is the way of ultimate reality, the way of the universe. One of its most characteristic symbols is another icon: the *yin/yang* polarity. The halves of the symbol are in tension, but they are not flatly opposed: each bends back on the other, interpenetrates the other, in the end to be resolved in a circle, the symbol of wholeness. In the Taoist perspective, even good and evil are not diametrically opposed—there are no sharp dichotomies. Taoism seeks attunement with nature and the cosmos, not dominance. Tao is the teacher of the soul. Jung defines the psychological meaning of the way of Tao to be "the method or conscious way by which to unite that which is separated."[18] Thomas Merton defined it as a "simplicity beyond opposites."

This path of personal development and the gradual embracing of transcending values and balancing dispositions has great significance also for the development of cultures, families, and all the myriad ways in which human beings organize themselves. In a world still rife with nationalism and ethnocentric narcissism, the question of bicultural or multicultural consciousness becomes critical. If the species and the planetary ecosystem are to survive and flourish, an evolutionary leap is necessary, something that promises more than the options of homogenization or coexistence—a new spiritual consciousness that can establish peaceful equilibrium while sustaining a *tension of opposites*.

Global theorists have instinctively grasped these basic values and incorporated them into a new social agenda that revises the old scientific view. Hazel Henderson calls hers "A Post-Cartesian Scientific Worldview." She describes six basic principles:

INTERCONNECTEDNESS: at every system level

REDISTRIBUTION: recycling of all elements and structures, reciprocity and sharing

HETERARCHY: networks and webs, intercommunication rather than hierarchies; interactive systems variables; self-organization; autopoesis, mutual causality

COMPLEMENTARITY: replacing either-or, dichotomous logics and
reframing with metalogics of "yin-yang" and "win-win" rather
than zero-sum games

UNCERTAINTY: a shift from static, homeostatic, and mechanistic
models to probabilistic, morphogenetic, oscillating, and cyclic
models; many viewpoints

CHANGE: change as fundamental, certainty as limited [19]

Others who interpret the paradigm shift in our time note the same
blurring of dichotomous logics, the rejection of individualism and
atomism, the displacement of hierarchy. Although these signs are
not universal by any means, they are clear indications that we are
entering a convergent rather than divergent phase in human and
social evolution. The Gaia hypothesis is only one of the many
frameworks for thinking that draw us inexorably toward a more
organic view of ourselves and the universe, a universe in which the
very properties of matter are a metaphor for our sacred origins in
the Mother of All.

But the old values and attitudes persist, sometimes with height-
ened intensity in the face of change and the fear it generates. Religious fundamentalism and anarchy feed the present state of
antagonism, hostility, fear, and aggression. Paramilitary groups fear
the "new world order" will mean the loss of a national ego. Islamic
fundamentalists foster an "either/or" vision of the world and see a
jihad as the only way to establish equilibrium. Bosnia, Rwanda,
Burma—the scenario is the same in all these places. Political extrem-
ists or ethnic rivals in a variety of cultures afflict us with draconian
policies and tactics. As in the spiritual life of the individual, these
are immature stages of development. They are all narcissistic and
ineffective responses to *difference*.

On the world stage, the progress in the Israeli/Palestinian relations demonstrates the first steps toward a new consciousness, an
effort to live in the *tension of opposites*. In North America we are
sometimes deluded into believing that the melting pot is real. Then
something like the O. J. Simpson trial happens, and we come face-
to-face with our differences. These differences go deeper than cen-

turies of discussions about race relations or colonialism or anthropological origins. *Difference* goes to the very core of the way we interpret and process—both cognitively and affectively—what we experience. The way we think and the way we feel make the difference.

Just as my trip to Japan opened my eyes to understanding myself as a Westerner, so the experience of the Simpson verdict helped me to understand myself better as a white North American woman. The aftermath itself came to symbolize more than the substance of the trial.

I remember the day of the verdict well, because of a parallel incident that was unforgettable. In the large medical facility where I was working, there were very few TVs connected to the cable system. As the time of the verdict drew closer, most of us were on lunch hour and scouted around for a TV that would be carrying the event live. The most accessible TV was in the large public lobby at the entrance of the clinic section of our building. About 12:55 P.M. an assortment of medical staff and patients gathered there to hear the expected verdict at 1 P.M. The lobby was large and could easily accommodate the additional folks. Anticipation was high and a communal atmosphere was evident, as often happens when one is about to participate in a shared moment of history. (As we learned later, we were doing what practically everyone else in America was doing at that moment, including the President and his staff, thousands of people on Times Square, in offices, homes, university auditoriums throughout the country.) Suddenly, at the very moment that the jury forewoman was opening the envelope, the director of the center burst into the lobby, shouting at the top of his voice that this was a "medical facility" and we should all go back to where we belonged. He was in such a frenzy of "white heat" that he went over to the TV and switched off the broadcast at the *very moment* when the verdict was to be read. I will never forget the look on his face or on the stunned faces of the people in the lobby, including some of the director's peers from other clinics. Some verbal outrage was expressed, but to no avail, so most of us streaked off to find someone with a radio.

When I thought about the performance of the director later, I thought what a perfect paradigm of Western, imperial, hierarchical behavior it was—at its worst. Full of patriarchal pompousness and disembodied knowing, this man was unable to respond and adapt to the feelings and desires of his own peers. Power and abstract thinking clouded his perception of an event that should have at least engaged his tolerance, if not his emotions.

When the verdict was read, I experienced a second, deeper shock. Later, after much rumination, the first event in the lobby gave me a context for understanding the verdict. I had followed the trial intermittently over its tortuous 265 days, 600 exhibits, and 126 witnesses. My Western logic convinced me that Simpson was guilty, that he was the only reasonable perpetrator. I was especially convinced by the strength of the DNA evidence and the over-whelming amount of circumstantial evidence. Scientifically, there could be no doubt, in my mind. His history of violent spousal abuse, his crazy ride on the Los Angeles freeway with a gun to his head, his reported confession—these bits of information sup-ported the scientific evidence. Computers had ruled out everyone else, or so it seemed to me.

But obviously, the jury reasoned differently. Simpson's domestic violence record was not relevant, but the history of bias of certain Los Angeles policemen was. I understood "justice" and "truth" as the sum of a thousand individual facts, all of which excluded other possibilities. The mostly black jury understood "justice" and "truth" as determined by a context that was completely untrustwor-thy. Being white and being schooled in "white thinking," I could separate my feelings from the events and evidence. The jury, being mostly black and schooled in "black thinking," could not separate feelings and experience from the evidence. "Reasonable doubt" was stretched beyond what I perceived as reasonable limits.

Here was a classic incidence of a clash between *experiential knowing* and *rational knowing*, between a disembodied, objec-tive analysis and an *embodied knowing* that spoke a truth that was larger than the mere question of a man's guilt. And yet, in the West-ern white mind, the individual is always more important than the group, so as a white American woman I cannot reconcile the image of the bodies of Nicole Simpson and Ron Goldman with the image of an O. J. Simpson who will no doubt spend a lifetime persuading us of his innocence.

Personally and politically we struggle to find the balance between the opposites, the equilibrium that does not sacrifice the good of either truth, but in a way that does not sacrifice people to a particular truth. So, on the world scene, we struggle to find a path between the way the United States understands human rights and the way China sees human rights. And while our principles cause us to agonize over the treatment of women in Asia or the Middle East, or the poor in Africa, our own social policies constantly subvert our principles of equality. These political and ethical differences are *growing edges* of spiritual transformation. They will continue to challenge us to stretch and expand our consciousness to new ways of knowing and being.

Perhaps the most serious danger is not the challenge of *difference*, but the loss of it. For all the obvious benefits of technology, we are beginning to see the cost. Technology and the growing hegemony of the Internet as a multipresent force can link us across cultures as never before—but it can also over time homogenize the pool of ideas. Media can stunt the creative imagination. The speed of transportation and electronic media, the geometric and geographic expansion of population brings us closer to those at a distance, but also creates new risks of rapacity and aggression. Monopoly, mergers, and the hoarding of resources and capital can shrink diversity and opportunity. Money can bring governments to a standstill or a crash; it can paralyze and poison democracy. Medicine, as it is delivered in some places today, can endanger health. The disappearance of the biodiversity of the rainforests endangers our future. Technology that spews gases into the atmosphere endangers our planet.

At the same time, new models of connectedness are emerging all around us. In the information era, access becomes more crucial than possession. Who will have access? What will this do to the economy? The Internet can move ideas faster than books; the hypertext of the World Wide Web is teaching us new, creative ways of shaping reality. Virtual community is replacing proximate, spatial community; subjectivity is no longer bounded by the skin and the brain. All of these transformations will have beneficial but destabilizing effects on our social arrangements and structures. To where shall we look for a principle, a motive of accountability?

We are like orphans, descended from a Great Mother, whose teaching and values we have forgotten. We are ignorant of our true ancestry. So we must think back through Eve, rethink the "fall," the eclipse, the fragmentation, the displacement. She demands recognition, and we must rediscover her. The paradigm of the future begins there. There we find the repressed Anima of the civilization, the imprisoned feminine reflected in the voices of the rising subjugated knowledges.

The image of Eve, symbol of our lost birthright of power and our lost connection with the Mother of All, will fade as the goddesses reappear—much as the huge sculpture of "Freedom," so dramatically feminine, burst out of the stony repression by China at Tiananmen Square in 1989. Only when we see ourselves reflected in the eyes of our True Mother will we see our "original face."

In his book on Kannon, the omnipresent Goddess of Mercy of Japan, Shun'ei Tagawa reminds us of how urgently we must develop the "eyes of Kannon," learn Kannon's way of looking at the world. This seeing is without preference or prejudice; it is not driven by self-centeredness or indulgence; it has empathy for all beings. It is the way of the Great Mother. According to Hindu cosmology, we are now living in the age of Kali, the Mistress of Time and Death, and therefore of Change—the Avenger of wounds to the Feminine.[20] These twin archetypes of Light and Darkness draw us inexorably toward the East—the place of Illumination on the Medicine Wheel of our Native American ancestors.

Afterword

My visit to Japan in late 1994 was the beginning of a journey that still continues—a journey into the depths of consciousness and the core of the differences between East and West, masculine and feminine, yin and yang. In the theophany of feminine archetypes in our time we are discovering our "original face" and a map for the future of the human community. There are spiritual and political lessons to be learned from the encounter with difference, and all those things we have forgotten, rejected, subjugated, or feared.

The spiritual quest is more than mastering a discipline or being faithful to a creed. It is not therapy and it is not technique. It is more than spiritual tourism. The spiritual quest meets us at the borders of our soul, in our encounters and experiences, in the struggles and surprises within and without. The personal life, the inner landscape, is a mirror of the social challenges and geopolitics of our time. It is a geography of soul with many hemispheres. To ignore one at the expense of the other is to risk never knowing who we really are, never discovering our true destiny.

I hope my reflections can be a catalyst for my readers to risk a journey into the unknown in their own lives, to seek out what is yet to be discovered or accepted.

With a profound bow of gratitude I thank my Japanese friends and spirit-guides who have enlightened me so much. And I beg their indulgence for anything that my first impressions may have missed or misunderstood.

Notes

Chapter One

1. This description is adapted in part from Peter Berger and Thomas Luckmann, *The Social Construction of Reality* (New York: Doubleday & Co., 1966), and Peter Berger, *The Sacred Canopy* (New York: Doubleday & Co., 1967).

2. Madonna Kolbenschlag, *Lost in the Land of Oz* (San Francisco: Harper & Row, 1988), 190 n. 26.

3. Ibid., 1–3.

4. Jordan Paper, *The Spirits Are Drunk: Comparative Approaches to Chinese Religion* (New York: SUNY Press: 1995), 229–30. See also E. T. C. Werner, *Myths and Legends of China* (New York: Dover, 1922, 1994); and Juliet Piggott, *Japanese Mythology* (New York: Peter Bedrick Books, 1969, 1982).

5. Demaris Wehr, "Religious and Social Dimensions of the Archetype," in *Feminist Archetypal Theory,* ed. Estella Lauter and Carol Schreier Rupprecht (Knoxville: University of Tennessee Press, 1985), 37.

6. Renate Höfer, *Die Hiobsbotschaft C. G. Jungs: Folgen sexuellen Missbrauchs* (Lüneburg: zu Klampen Verlag GbR, 1993).

7. Luce Irigaray, quoted in Madonna Kolbenschlag, *Lost in the Land of Oz,* 61.

8. Adrienne Rich, *On Lies, Secrets and Silence: Selected Prose, 1966–1978* (New York: W. W. Norton & Co., 1979), 187.

9. Ann and Barry Ulanov, *Transforming Sexuality: The Archetypal World of Anima and Animus* (Boston and London: Shambhala, 1995), 29.

10. Mark Thompson, *Gay Soul: Finding the Heart of Gay Spirit and Nature* (San Francisco: HarperSan Francisco, 1990), 3.

Chapter Two

1. D. T. Suzuki, *Japanese Spirituality*, trans. Norman Woddell (New York and London: Greenwood Press, 1988, 1972), 17–23.

2. Rev. Shun'ei Tagawa is chief abbot of the Kofukuji Temple in Nara. He is the author of a book explaining Yuishiki Buddhism, *Yuishiki Jusho* (Japan: Shunshusha, 1989, 1994), and one on the place of Kannon in Yuishiki, *Kannon Bukkyo No Kokoro* (Japan: Shunshusha, 1993). He graduated in psychology from Ritsumeikan University in Kyoto and is familiar with current trends in psychology in the West.

3. Madonna Kolbenschlag, "The God-Myth Scale: Measuring the God-Representation" (diss., Fielding Institute, Santa Barbara, CA, 1992).

4. Dialog between Rev. Shun'ei Tagawa and Madonna Kolbenschlag, Kofukuji Temple, Nara, Japan, November 20, 1994. Mr. Paul McGrath and Ms. Keiko Morita also participated and translated.

5. Rev. Shun'ei Tagawa, *Kannon Bukkyo No Kokoro*.

6. H. Byron Earhart, *Religions of Japan: Many Traditions Within One Sacred Way* (San Francisco: Harper & Row, 1984), 50–51.

7. Takeo Doi, *The Anatomy of Self: The Individual Versus Society*, trans. Mark Harbison (Tokyo and New York: Kodansha International, 1985), 148.

8. Huston Smith, *The World's Religions* (San Francisco: HarperSan Francisco, 1991, 1958), 212.

9. Clark B. Offner, *Modern Japanese Religions: With Special Emphasis upon Their Doctrines of Healing* (New York: Twayne Publishers, 1963), 140.

10. Kosuke Koyama, *Mount Fuji and Mount Sinai: A Critique of Idols* (Maryknoll, NY: Orbis Books, 1984), 152.

11. Ibid., 240.

12. D. Miller, *The New Polytheism* (New York: Harper & Row, 1974) quoted in Frank Johnson, "The Western Concept of Self," in *Culture and Self: Asian and Western Perspectives,* ed. A. Marsella, G. DeVos, and F. Hsu (New York and London: Tavistock, 1985), 116.

13. Morris Berman, *The Reenchantment of the World* (Ithaca, NY, and London: Cornell University Press, 1981).

14. From personal notes of a talk by Jacques Lacan, ca. 1972.

15. Sumiko Iwao, *The Japanese Woman: Traditional Image and Changing Reality* (New York: Free Press, 1993), 282.

16. E. Sampson, "The Decentralization of Identity," *American Psychologist* 40/11 (1985): 1203.

17. Takeo Doi, *The Anatomy of Self,* 23ff., 42–43.

18. George DeVos, "Dimensions of the Self in Japanese Culture," in *Culture and Self,* ed. A. Marsella et al., 25–53.

19. Frank Johnson, "The Western Concept of Self," in *Culture and Self,* ed. A. Marsella et al., 118.

20. Kakuzo Okakura, *The Book of Tea* (Tokyo and New York: Kodansha International, 1989).

21. Raimundo Panikkar, *The Silence of God: The Answer of Buddha,* trans. Robert Barr (Maryknoll, NY: Orbis Books, 1989), 174–75.

22. C. G. Jung, "Commentary on the Golden Flower," in *The Secret of the Golden Flower: A Chinese Book of Life,* trans. Richard Wilhelm (San Diego, New York, London: Harcourt Brace Jovanovich, 1962, 1931), 128.

Chapter Three

1. Sumiko Iwao, *The Japanese Woman,* 69–73.

2. Tanaka Mitsu, in *The Hidden Sun: Women of Modern Japan,* ed. Dorothy Robins-Mowry (Boulder, CO: Westview Press, 1983).

3. Yukiko Tanaka, *This Kind of Woman: Ten Stories by Japanese Women Writers, 1960–1976* (Stanford, CA: Stanford University Press, 1982), xiii.

4. Kathryn Ann Tsai, *Lives of the Nuns: Biographies of Chinese Buddhist Nuns from the Fourth to Sixth Centuries* (Honolulu: University of Hawaii Press, 1994).

5. Elizabeth Petroff, "The Beguines in Medieval Europe: An Expression of Feminine Spirituality," in *The Goddess Re-Awakening: The Feminine Principle Today,* ed. Shirley Nicholson (Wheaton, IL: Theosophical Publishing House, 1989), 199. See also Elizabeth Petroff, ed., *Medieval Women's Visionary Literature* (New York: Oxford University Press, 1986), and Fiona Bowie, ed., *Beguine Spirituality* (New York: Crossroad, 1990), which has a good bibliography.

6. Nicholas Bornoff, *Pink Samurai: Love, Marriage & Sex in Contemporary Japan* (New York: Simon & Schuster, 1991), 425ff., and Ian Buruma, *Behind the Mask* (New York: Pantheon Books, 1984), 128ff.

7. Claude Lévi-Strauss, quoted in Ian Buruma, *Behind the Mask*, 115.

8. Ian Buruma, *Behind the Mask*, 127.

9. John D'Emilio, "Capitalism and Gay Identity," in *Powers of Desire: The Politics of Sexuality*, ed. Ann Snitow, Christine Stansell, and Sharon Thompson (New York: Monthly Review Press, 1983), 102, 105.

10. Saul Rosenzweig, "Sexual Autonomy as an Evolutionary Attainment," in *Sexual Behavior: Critical Issues in 1970s*, ed. J. Zubin and J. Money (Baltimore and London: Johns Hopkins University Press, 1973), 214–15.

11. These terms originated with Sandra Lipsitz Bem, *The Lenses of Gender: Transforming the Debate on Sexual Inequality* (New Haven and London: Yale University Press, 1993). See also Jeffrey Weeks, *Sexuality* (London and New York: Tavistock Publications, 1986).

12. E. O. Wilson, quoted in Jeffrey Weeks, *Sexuality,* 49.

13. Sandra Lipsitz Bem, *Lenses of Gender.*

14. See Jean Baker Miller's landmark work, *Toward a New Psychology of Women* (Boston: Beacon Press, 2d ed., 1986).

15. Sandra Lipsitz Bem, *Lenses of Gender*, 155–57.

16. Ann and Barry Ulanov, *Transforming Sexuality*, 213.

17. Ibid., 215.

18. Cathy Davidson, *36 Views of Mount Fuji: On Finding Myself in Japan* (New York: Dutton, 1993), 81–82.

19. Elizabeth Petroff, "The Beguines in Medieval Europe," in *The Goddess Re-Awakening,* ed. Nicholson, 199.

20. Héléne Cixous, ibid., 193–94.

Chapter Four

1. P. Teilhard de Chardin, quoted in Mary and Ellen Lukas, *Teilhard* (Garden City, NY: Doubleday, 1977), 92.

2. Ibid., 79.

3. P. Teilhard de Chardin, quoted in Thomas King, *Teilhard de Chardin* (Wilmington, DE: Michael Glazier, 1988), 153.

4. P. Teilhard de Chardin, "The Spiritual Contribution of the Far East," in *Toward the Future* (New York and London: Harcourt Brace Jovanovich, 1975), 137–39.

5. Ibid., 142.

6. Ibid., 144–45.

7. P. Teilhard de Chardin, "My Fundamental Vision," in *Toward the Future*, 203. See also P. Teilhard de Chardin, *How I Believe*, trans. René Hague (New York: Harper & Row, 1969), 68–69.

8. P. Teilhard de Chardin, *The Heart of Matter*, trans. René Hague (New York and London: Harcourt Brace Jovanovich, 1978), 59.

9. Lucile Swan, *P. Teilhard de Chardin*, in Thomas King, *Teilhard de Chardin*, 168, 169.

10. P. Teilhard de Chardin, in Henri de Lubac, *The Eternal Feminine: A Study on the Poem by Teilhard de Chardin* (New York: Harper & Row, 1971), 57.

11. P. Teilhard de Chardin, "The Evolution of Chastity," in *Toward the Future*, 60–87.

12. Mary and Ellen Lukas, *Teilhard*, 135.

13. P. Teilhard de Chardin, *Activation of Energy*, trans. René Hague (New York and London: Harcourt Brace Jovanovich, 1970), 392.

14. See Robert Stoller, in "Myth of Man-Kind," chap. 3 of *Lost in the Land of Oz*, by Madonna Kolbenschlag.

15. Harold Talbot, "The Jesus Lama: Thomas Merton in the Himalayas," interview in *Tricycle* (Summer, 1992): 14–24.

16. See "Myth of Man-Kind," chap. 3 of *Lost in the Land of Oz*, by Madonna Kolbenschlag.

17. Thomas Merton, letter to Victor Hammer, May 14, 1959, cited *Thomas Merton: Spiritual Master – The Essential Writings*, ed. Lawrence Cunningham (New York and Mahwah, NJ: Paulist Press, 1992), 257.

18. Thomas Merton, "Hagia Sophia," in *Thomas Merton*, ed. Lawrence Cunningham, 258–64.

19. Thomas Merton, "Conjectures of a Guilty Bystander," in *Thomas Merton*, ed. Lawrence Cunningham, 144.

20. Thomas Merton, letter to Rosemary Ruether, February 14, 1967, in *The Hidden Ground of Love: Letters of Thomas Merton on Religious Experience and Social Concerns* (New York: Farrar, Straus, Giroux, 1985), 501.

21. William Shannon, *Silent Lamp: The Thomas Merton Story* (New York: Crossroad, 1993), 279–81.

22. Thomas Merton, *Zen and the Birds of Appetite* (New York: New Directions, 1968), 140.

23. Thomas Merton, *Asian Journal* (New York: New Directions, 1973, 1975).

24. C. G. Jung has an extended commentary in *Psychology and the East*, trans. R. F. C. Hull (Princeton, NJ: Princeton University Press, 1978), 59–76.

25. Joseph Campbell, *The Masks of God: Creative Mythology* (New York: Penguin Books, 1968), 420ff.

Chapter Five

1. Cathy Davidson, *36 Views of Mount Fuji*, 53.

2. David Goodman and Masanori Miyazawa, *Jews in the Japanese Mind* (New York: Free Press, 1995), quoted in *Fortune* (March 20, 1995): 137.

3. Louis Kraar, in *Fortune* (March 20, 1995): 136.

4. Nakasone Yasuhiro, quoted in Marilyn Ivy, "Critical Texts, Mass Artifacts: The Consumption of Knowledge in Postmodern Japan," in *Postmodernism and Japan,* ed. Miyoshi and Harootunian (Durham, NC: Duke University Press, 1989).

5. Goodman and Miyazawa, *Jews in the Japanese Mind.*

6. Tsushima Yuko, "The Possibility of Imagination in These Islands," *Boundary* 2, 21:1 (Spring 1994): 191–97.

7. Cathy Davidson, *36 Views of Mount Fuji*, 198.

8. Avrion Mitchison, "Will We Survive?" *Scientific American* 269/3 (September 1993): 136–44.

9. Gregory Bateson and Mary Catherine Bateson, *Angels Fear: Towards an Epistemology of the Sacred* (New York: Macmillan, 1987), 18.

10. Mary Catherine Bateson, *Peripheral Visions: Learning Along the Way* (New York: HarperCollins, 1994), 46–47.

11. Ibid., 8.

12. Ibid., 43–44.

13. Mary Catherine Bateson, *With a Daughter's Eye: A Memoir of*

Margaret Mead and Gregory Bateson (New York: HarperPerennial, 1994), 116.

14. Mary Catherine Bateson, *Composing a Life* (New York: Atlantic Monthly Press, 1989), 63.

15. Mary Catherine Bateson, *Peripheral Visions*, 81.

16. Ibid., 84.

17. Ibid., 83.

18. Joe Flower, "Differences Make a Difference," *Healthcare Forum Journal* (September-October 1992): 64.

19. Ibid., 64.

20. Mary Catherine Bateson, *Composing a Life*, 9–10, 13–14.

21. Barbara Christian, "Remembering Audre Lorde," in *Women's Review of Books* 10:6 (March 1993): 5.

22. Ibid.

23. Audre Lorde, "Among Ourselves," *A Burst of Light* (Ithaca, NY: Firebrand Books, 1988).

24. Audre Lorde, "Uses of the Erotic," in *Weaving the Visions*, ed. J. Plaskow and Carol Christ (San Francisco: Harper & Row, 1989), 209.

25. Audre Lorde, "Age, Race, Sex and Class" from *Sister/Outsider*, quoted in Barbara Christian, "Remembering Audre Lorde," 5.

26. Joanna Macy, *Dharma and Development: Religion as Resource in the Sarvodaya Self-Help Movement* (West Hartford, CT: Kumarian Press, 1983), 9.

27. Ibid., 19–20.

28. Joanna Macy, *World as Lover, World as Self* (Berkeley, CA: Parallax Press, 1991), 54.

29. Mary Catherine Bateson, *Peripheral Visions*, 179.

30. Joanna Macy, *World as Lover, World as Self*, 58.

31. Ibid., 63.

32. Joanna Macy, "Awakening to the Ecological Self," in *Healing the Wounds: The Promise of Ecofeminism*, ed. Judith Plant (Philadelphia: New Society Publisher, 1989), 205.

33. Joanna Macy, *World as Lover, World as Self*, 120–21.

34. Joanna Macy, personal correspondence, September 22, 1995.

35. P. Teilhand de Chardin, *Human Energy*, trans. J. M. Cohen (New York: Harcourt Brace Jovanovich, 1969), 85.

36. Marilyn Ivy, "Critical Texts," 26, 29.

37. Manami Suzuki, "Seeds that Bear Fruit" in *Reclaim the Earth*, ed. L. Caldecott and S. Leland (London: Women's Press, 1983), 87.

38. Joanna Macy, "Awakening to the Ecological Self," 206.

39. Ibid., 202.

Chapter Six

1. Ian Buruma, *Behind the Mask,* 115.

2. Merlin Stone, *Ancient Mirrors of Womanhood* (Village Station, NY: New Sibylline Books, 1979), 1:29.

3. Dialog in Nara, Japan between Rev. Shun'ei Tagawa and Madonna Kolbenschlag, Kofukuji Temple, November 20, 1994. Translation summary of Rev. Tagawa's *Kannon Bukkyo No Kokoro* by Akihide Mazutani, October 1995.

4. David Toolan, *Facing West from California's Shores* (New York: Crossroad, 1987), 74.

5. Ann Baring and Jules Cashford, *The Myth of the Goddess: Evolution of an Image* (New York: Viking, 1991), 609ff.

6. A. Baring and J. Cashford, *The Myth of the Goddess,* 613.

7. Elaine Pagels, cited in A. Baring and J. Cashford, *The Myth of the Goddess,* 619.

8. A. Baring and J. Cashford, *The Myth of the Goddess,* 621.

9. Barbara Newman, *Sister of Wisdom: St. Hildegard's Theology of the Feminine* (Berkeley, CA: University of California Press, 1987), 46ff.

10. This socialization process is well documented in recent studies by the American Association of University Women, in studies like *The Cost of Competence* by B. Silverstein and D. Perlick; *"Women's Ways of Knowing* by M. Belenky, N. Goldberger, et al.; and *School Girls* by Peggy Orenstein. I have described the complementary process of male socialization in "The Myth of Man-Kind," chap. 3 in *Lost in the Land of Oz.*

11. Tataya Mato, *The Black Madonna Within* (Chicago: Open Court, 1994).

12. Michael Grosso, quoted in Andrea Young, "Visions of the Virgin," *Common Boundary* (May/June 1994): 41.

13. Russell Means, interview by John Edgar Wideman, *Modern Maturity* (September-October 1995): 70–71.

14. David K. Reynolds, *Morita Psychotherapy* (Berkeley, CA: University of California Press, 1976), 110.

15. Quoted in James Hall, M.D., *The Jungian Experience* (Toronto: Inner City Books), 87.

16. Explicated in Edward Edinger's *The Mystery of the Conjunctio: Alchemical Image of Individuation* (Toronto: Inner City Books, 1994).

17. Merlin Stone, *Ancient Mirrors of Womanhood*, 25.

18. C. G. Jung, *Psychology and the East*, 23.

19. Hazel Henderson, *Paradigms in Progress: Life Beyond Economics* (San Francisco: Berrett-Koehler, 1991, 1995), 52, 66.

20. Shun'ei Tagawa, *Kannon Bukkyo No Kokoro*, and letter, January 4, 1995. Also, Hallie Iglehart Austen, *The Heart of the Goddess* (Berkeley, CA: Wingbow, 1990), 78.

About the Author

MADONNA KOLBENSCHLAG is a clinical psychologist on the staff of the West Virginia University Health Services in Morgantown, WV, and an associate professor of behavioral medicine and psychiatry. She is also currently a Women's Commissioner for the State of West Virginia.

Dr. Kolbenschlag is best known as a social philosopher and author of six books. She has gained a national and international reputation as a writer and lecturer on women's development and gender issues, on cultural analysis and public policy, and on spirituality and religious affairs. Her first book, *Kiss Sleeping Beauty Good-Bye,* has been translated into five languages. She is also the author of *Lost in the Land of Oz,* recently published in a new expanded edition by Crossroad, and of *Eastward Toward Eve.* She has lectured throughout the United States and in many foreign countries, including Europe, Latin America, Japan, and Ireland.

Dr. Kolbenschlag studied for her first doctorate in literature at the University of Notre Dame (1973) and received her second doctorate in clinical psychology from the Fielding Institute (1992). In the 1970s she was a professor of American Studies at the University of Notre Dame and lectured at Loyola University in Chicago. In the 1980s she held a position as legislative aide and research consultant in the U.S. House of Representatives in Washington, DC. in addition, Dr. Kolbenschlag was a senior fellow at the Woodstock Theological Center, a research institute of Georgetown University, Washington, DC.

Dr. Kolbenschlag is currently a member of the governing board of the interfaith Center for Corporate Responsibility in New York, and has lectured for many universities and professional organizations. She is the author of many scholarly and public interest articles.

Of Related Interest

Madonna Kolbenschlag

Lost in the Land of Oz

*Befriending Your Inner Orphan
and Heading for Home*

Using myth, fairy tale, and story, Madonna Kolbenschlag reevaluates the American dream and offers a new paradigm of spiritual awareness and union with one another.

"This is must reading!"
— Anne Wilson Schaef

"An important contribution to gender studies."
— Library Journal

0-8245-1402-5 $13.95 pb

Beatrice Bruteau

What We Can Learn from the East

Beatrice Bruteau offers perspectives and practices from Eastern wisdom sources that have parallels in Christianity so that Christians can adapt or adopt them and deepen their own experiences. She also presents challenging ideas from the East that are at variance with usual Christian beliefs in order to stimulate fresh thinking and new insights.

0-8245-1457-2 $11.95 pb

*At your bookstore, or directly
from the Crossroad Publishing Company,
370 Lexington Avenue,
New York, NY 10017.
Please send payment with order,
including $3.00 for the first book
plus $1.00 for each additional book
to cover shipping and handling fees.
Thank you.*